The Unknown Testament

The Unknown Testament

LOWELL L. BENNION

Deseret Book Company
Salt Lake City, Utah

No part of this book may be reproduced in any
form or by any means without permission in writing
from the publisher, Deseret Book Company,
P.O. Box 30178, Salt Lake City, Utah 84130.
Deseret Book is a registered trademark of
Deseret Book Company.

First printing February 1988

Library of Congress Cataloging-in-Publication Data

Bennion, Lowell Lindsay, 1908-
  The unknown testament.

  Includes index.
  1. Bible. O.T.—Criticism, interpretation, etc.
2. Church of Jesus Christ of Latter-day Saints—
Doctrines. 3. Mormon Church—Doctrines. I. Title.
BS1171.2.B46 1988   221.6   87-33193
ISBN 0-87579-131-X

CONTENTS

PART III: OLD TESTAMENT CONTRIBUTIONS TO THE RELIGIOUS LIFE

PART IV: SOCIAL PHILOSOPHY IN THE OLD TESTAMENT

Part I

THE BOOK

Chapter 1
THE UNKNOWN SCRIPTURE

The Old Testament is the least known and least understood of the standard works of The Church of Jesus Christ of Latter-day Saints. This is unfortunate, because the Old Testament commends itself to us in many ways. It has great historical interest, covering the longest period of time in religious history. From a literary point of view, the King James Version is unequalled in English prose. Most important, it is the fountainhead of many basic religious concepts that are part of our Judeo-Christian legacy. Its teachings have profoundly influenced the culture, the legal institutions, and the political structure of Western civilization.

Why is the Old Testament so little read and appreciated? One reason is that its very age creates problems. To understand it presupposes some knowledge of the time and circumstances of its writing and of the authors and their audience and purpose. The prophets were speaking in their own century to their own people in critical historical situations. Some of their teachings have local and temporary meaning only; others have universal and enduring value. It is not always easy to distinguish between the two, but the Old Testament cannot be

3

understood apart from the times and circumstances in which its writings were produced. This does not require a specialist's knowledge, of course; many excellent commentaries will provide a perfectly adequate introduction.

A second problem with understanding the Old Testament is its structure. People habitually read a book from cover to cover, from beginning to end; but the Old Testament was not written as a single book. Instead, it is a collection of thirty-nine separate writings brought together into a single volume centuries after they were written. It is more like a shelf of books in a library, arranged neither chronologically nor alphabetically. Proverbs and Psalms are themselves collections of writings composed over centuries. (The next chapter suggests a more helpful reading order than beginning to end.)

Some Christians have not been interested in the Old Testament for its own sake but only because it predicts the coming of Jesus Christ. Although this interest is legitimate, it can be so powerful that they may relate passages to the Savior that do not apply to him. This might be called "Christianizing" the Old Testament, a practice understandably disturbing to Jewish scholars. Certainly some passages in the Old Testament that predict the coming of a Messiah are admirably fulfilled by Christ. Moreover, Jesus, Peter, and Paul quote the Old Testament to establish the Christian faith. But looking only for Christian-related passages in the Old Testament will divert our attention from many other religious concepts that are unique to that scripture and of great importance and value.

Latter-day Saints have a strong propensity to "Mormonize" the Old Testament because of the added knowledge of Christ's mission found in the Book of Mormon and the book of Moses. The book of Moses, a revelation to Joseph Smith, greatly expands Christ's central premortal role in the creation and redemption of human-

4

kind. We have a right to enlarge our Christian understanding by reference to these other scriptures, but I
believe we should recognize them for what they are—
additional sources of knowledge—and not assume that
they are part of the Old Testament as we have received
it.

Each scripture is unique. Each has its original and
special contribution to make. Each should be studied and
appreciated for what it is. Each should be respected for
its own integrity.

A fourth cause of difficulty in understanding the Old
Testament is the perception of some modern readers that
every line of the Bible except mistranslations is divine.
The Old Testament, I believe, contains much that reflects
the mind and will of God, especially the writings of the
prophets who were confident that they spoke for him and
whose thoughts bear witness to me of divine influence.
But there are other writings—narrations, stories, histo-
ries, proverbs, and psalms—that have value but are less
inspired. One of the Old Testament books, the Song of
Solomon, is a romantic love song that seems out of place
in a religious text. It became part of the canon only by
the somewhat strained reasoning that it was an allegory
of the love God and Israel had for each other. Another
work, Ecclesiastes, though beautifully written, is quite
foreign to the faith and optimism of the Old Testament
as a whole. In the narrative and historical books, authors
occasionally justify Israel's actions by explaining that
God willed them, even though those actions are unworthy of the Deity taught by the prophets and Jesus.

In short, much of the Old Testament is valid for us
today, but some of it is an expression of different conditions, attitudes, and a more limited understanding of
the will of God. One indication of its limitations is that
the Hebrew prophets had to correct mistaken ideas of
their own people about the character and will of God, as

5

the book of Jonah does. It is surely consistent to believe that these comparatively more enlightened prophets would also welcome further light and knowledge.

The law of Moses is a splendid achievement for its day. Much of it, such as the Decalogue, or Ten Commandments, is equally valid for us. Other parts — dietary laws, hygienic rules, and sacrifices — are much less relevant, even among modern Jews.

The Old Testament is a wonderfully honest and human record as well as inspired of God. Its humanity and divinity co-mingle in a fascinating record. It works best when it is read for its own sake, not as something it is not.

Chapter 2

THE BOOKS OF THE OLD TESTAMENT

The Old Testament was probably over a thousand years in the making. It did not come into its present form until the end of the first century A.D. The Jewish Old Testament developed in three groupings: the Law (Torah or Pentateuch), the Prophets, and the Writings.

The Law, ascribed to Moses and consisting of Genesis, Exodus, Leviticus, Numbers, and Deuteronomy, had become scripture for the Jews by 400 B.C. It was held to be the most authoritative and sacred part of the Old Testament.

The second group, the Prophets, came in two divisions: the former and the latter prophets. The former prophets, which are narrative, historical works, consist of Joshua, Judges, 1 and 2 Samuel, and 1 and 2 Kings. The latter prophets consist of fifteen truly prophetic books: the three great prophets (Isaiah, Jeremiah, and Ezekiel) and the twelve "minor" prophets (Amos, Hosea, Micah, Zephaniah, Nahum, Habakkuk, Obadiah, Haggai, Zechariah, Malachi, Joel, and Jonah). They were accepted as scripture about 200 B.C.

The third group, the Writings, consists of Psalms, Proverbs, Job, the Song of Solomon, Ruth, Lamentations, Ecclesiastes, Esther, Daniel, 1 and 2 Chronicles, Ezra, and Nehemiah. They did not become part of the Jewish canon until about A.D. 70.

When a lawyer asked Jesus, "Master, which is the great commandment in the law?" Jesus quoted the commandments to love God and love one's neighbor, for "on these two commandments hang all the law and the prophets." (Matt. 22:26-40.) By that, he meant the accepted scripture of the day. He did not add the Writings because they were not yet part of the Old Testament canon.

Another group of books, the Apocrypha, were part of the Jewish canon but did not have the authority of the thirty-nine books mentioned above. Written between 200 B.C. and the fall of Jerusalem in A.D. 70, they contain important historical and human-interest material. Catholics from time to time have included these books in some of their editions of the Bible, while Protestants have generally excluded them. Joseph Smith's family Bible contained them; but when he was working on his new translation of the Bible, he received a revelation instructing him:

> There are many things contained therein that are true, and it is mostly translated correctly;
> There are many things contained therein that are not true, which are interpolations by the hands of men.
> Verily, I say unto you, that it is not needful that the Apocrypha should be translated.
> Therefore, whoso readeth it, let him understand, for the Spirit manifesteth truth. (D&C 9:1-4.)

The Apocrypha is readily available today in a variety of translations, either as a separate publication or as part of a standard edition of the Bible. Its books consist of Tobit (200 B.C.), Ecclesiasticus, or the Wisdom of Jesus, the Son of Sirach (175 B.C.), Song of the Three Holy Children (150 B.C.), 1 and 2 Esdras, Judith (150 B.C.), Prayer of Manasses (150-100 B.C.), Additions to Esther (100 B.C.), the History of Susanna (100-75 B.C.), Bel and the Dragon (100-75 B.C.), 1 Maccabees (100-75 B.C.), 2 Maccabees (75-65 B.C.), and the Wisdom of Solomon (A.D. 38-41).

HOW TO READ THE OLD TESTAMENT

Each book of the Old Testament should be read as a separate work along with some information about its background, author (if known), and content. Any good Bible commentary will give this information. (Appendix A, pp. 153-57, contains a brief description of each of the thirty-nine books.) The first books of the Bible, those found in the Law and the former Prophets, can be read in the order in which they are printed with the exception that Leviticus and Numbers should be reversed because Numbers continues the account recorded in Exodus.

The end of David's life and the reign of Solomon are described in 2 Kings, chapters 1 through 15. The remainder of 1 Kings and all of 2 Kings deal with the divided kingdoms of Israel and Judah and describe the conditions in which the prophets of Israel — Elijah, Elisha, and the fifteen writing prophets — declare their messages. The prophetic books should be read along with 1 and 2 Kings in this order: Zephaniah, Jeremiah, Nahum, Habakkuk, Ezekiel, Haggai, Zechariah, Nehemiah, Obadiah, Joel, Malachi, and Jonah. Table 1, "A Chronology of the Prophets" (page 10) gives the approximate dates of the historical outline.

The third group of books, the Writings, can be read as a group, again considering each book as a unit with an introduction to supply context. Proverbs, Ecclesiastes, and Job, collectively, are called Wisdom Literature and may be read as a group. Proverbs is optimistic, full

TABLE 1. CHRONOLOGY OF THE PROPHETS

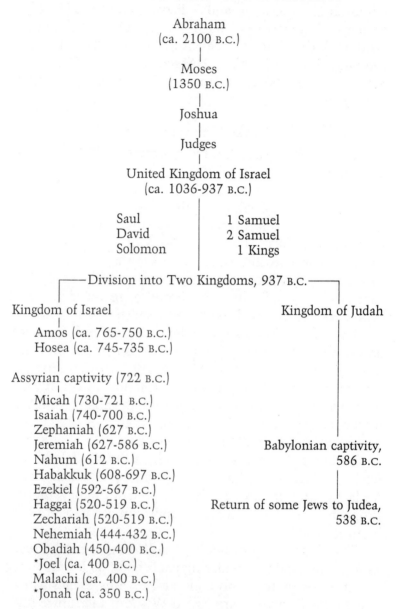

Abraham
(ca. 2100 B.C.)

Moses
(1350 B.C.)

Joshua

Judges

United Kingdom of Israel
(ca. 1036-937 B.C.)

Saul	1 Samuel
David	2 Samuel
Solomon	1 Kings

———Division into Two Kingdoms, 937 B.C.———

Kingdom of Israel   Kingdom of Judah

Amos (ca. 765-750 B.C.)
Hosea (ca. 745-735 B.C.)

Assyrian captivity (722 B.C.)

Micah (730-721 B.C.)
Isaiah (740-700 B.C.)
Zephaniah (627 B.C.)
Jeremiah (627-586 B.C.)   Babylonian captivity,
Nahum (612 B.C.)   586 B.C.
Habakkuk (608-697 B.C.)
Ezekiel (592-567 B.C.)
Haggai (520-519 B.C.)   Return of some Jews to Judea,
Zechariah (520-519 B.C.)   538 B.C.
Nehemiah (444-432 B.C.)
Obadiah (450-400 B.C.)
*Joel (ca. 400 B.C.)
Malachi (ca. 400 B.C.)
*Jonah (ca. 350 B.C.)

*Dated much earlier by a minority of scholars

of faith, purpose, and motivation, while Ecclesiastes is pessimistic, realistic, and disillusioned. They balance each other. Job is a classic work, profound and beautifully written.

Psalms can be read any time for meditation and worship.

Esther and Ruth, written with settings centuries apart, tell the stories of two revered women in the history of Israel and Judah. Ruth, a Moabite, was the foremother of David. Esther saved her people from destruction during the Babylonian captivity.

Daniel is an inspiring historical narrative for Jews during a period of captivity and discouragement, and includes prophecies as well.

Ezra and Nehemiah give insight into the building of a new temple and the reestablishment of the religion and people of Judah after their return from the Babylonian captivity in 538 B.C. Ezra was the religious leader, Nehemiah, the political leader.

The books of 1 and 2 Chronicles cover the history of the Old Testament from the creation (briefly) to the Babylonian captivity, 586 B.C. Probably written at the time of Ezra and Nehemiah, these two books place special emphasis on the history of Judah and temple building.

The Song of Solomon might be read whenever you are in a romantic or literary mood.

The remaining chapters in this book will not discuss each book in sequence. Instead, they will develop some basic concepts of Old Testament religion that have value for us.

Chapter 3

THE BIBLE AS LITERATURE

The ancient Israelites excelled in literature but turned away from creative efforts in the visual arts of painting and sculpture. With the exception of their temple, they did not produce architectural monuments that could be ranked with those of Greece, Egypt, or other Mediterranean countries.

The first reason for this was a religious prohibition against art. The Israelites were surrounded in Canaan by people who worshipped gods carved from wood and stone. As the Old Testament makes clear, this chosen people could be easily seduced to worship visual objects. The golden calf incident is only one event in a long history of dallying with idolatry. (Ex. 32.) Basic to the Decalogue was the warning against graven images:

> Thou shalt have no other gods before me.
> Thou shalt not make unto thee any graven image, or any likeness of any thing that is in heaven above, or that is in the earth beneath, or that is in the water under the earth:
> Thou shalt not bow down thyself to them, nor serve them. (Ex. 20:3-5.)

Clearly, no matter what rationale might be used for

13

creating an image, the Lord was interested in removing a temptation. The Greek glorification of human beings and individual arts produced an irreplaceable aesthetic and philosophical heritage for the western world. Moses and the other prophets, in turning away from the images of this world, focused attention on an even more important aspect of human life: our relationship to Deity and the invisible realities of the spiritual life.

A second reason why the Israelites produced no great visual arts lies in the accidents of its history. During the patriarchal period, the Hebrews were semi-nomads, then slaves in Egypt, then an army in Canaan. During these centuries, they could tell stories, sing hymns, and chant poetry — portable artifacts that they carried in their minds. However, such mobility would have made it difficult to produce permanent art objects. Even their literature was often expressed and transmitted orally.

This does not mean, however, that the Israelites had no aesthetic life. People have aesthetic feelings that call for expression in some way, and the Israelites of antiquity expressed their aesthetics very effectively in words. Their literature is profoundly beautiful.

I, probably like you, do not read Hebrew. I feel fortunate that in the King James Version of the Bible we have an aesthetic achievement that must match, in its own way, the achievement of the first writers. Four characteristics of the Old Testament suggest to me that it is a supreme literary achievement: its thematic significance, the concreteness and specificity of its imagery, its parallelism, and the diversity of forms it contains.

THEMATIC SIGNIFICANCE

Great literature discusses ideas of significance. Old Testament writers did not deal with trivia and superficialities, but struggled to define ideas of supreme importance: God's will and his ways, his concern for human beings and for human destiny, and the nature of truth. Again and again, they return to major questions: Why do nations rise and fall? What is good and evil? Why do the innocent suffer? What is our obligation to our neighbors and to society? Where is wisdom to be found? What is acceptable worship to our God?

In dealing with these themes, the Old Testament presents truth — not only the factual events of a particular king's reign or the outcome of a particular battle, but the truth of meaning. From the Old Testament, we understand not only *what* happened but the *significance* of what happened.

For instance, we are all familiar with the Parable of the Good Samaritan. Jesus observed life keenly and had great insight into people's motives. Certainly, he and his listeners knew of instances when travelers had been attacked and robbed, perhaps even killed; of other instances when a supposedly pious person had behaved in a selfish, perhaps openly exploitive, way; and of still other instances when an unlikely individual within a family or a community had stepped forward in a time of need. Perhaps there had never been an instance when an unfortunate traveler had been ignored by ecclesiastical officials and succored by an outcast, but the separate details of this parable were all true to life and could have happened just as Jesus described them. However, I believe that this parable was constructed by the genius of his creative mind in just this way to drive home a great idea. Perhaps if he had related "factual" details that would likely have been more common — that the traveler was discovered by a group of merchants traveling together, for instance — the significant truth of this parable would have been diluted.

In the same way, we must consider the facts and the truth of the Old Testament and some of its narratives. For instance, the debate over the accuracy of the details in the book of Job and the book of Jonah is centuries old. We will never have enough information to know if a man could survive three days inside a great fish, if Nineveh archives would show mass repentance on such-and-such a date, or if vines in Nineveh's ecology are capable of overnight growth and are particularly susceptible to large worms. These *facts* are beyond us, but the *truth* of Jonah's attempts at disobedience, of God's power, and of divine concern for all human beings does not depend on such factual accuracy. It could have happened just as the author relates, but the purposeful creativity of the story contains transcendent truths.

VIVID IMAGERY

Old Testament writings are rich with images that are concrete, vivid, and earthy. The language is not abstract philosophizing or abstruse jargon, but is drawn directly from everyday experiences. Listeners could touch and see the things the writers were talking about. Note the language of Isaiah:

> Hear, O heavens, and give ear, O earth: for the Lord hath spoken, I have nourished and brought up children, and they have rebelled against me.
>
> The ox knoweth his owner, and the ass his master's crib: but Israel doth not know, my people doth not consider. (Isa. 1:2-3.)

Here Isaiah holds up Israel's deliberate dullness against the contrasting understanding of the reputedly stupid ox and the stubborn donkey. A few verses later, he paints a graphic picture of the consequence of Israel's deliberate lack of understanding, speaking in the present tense as though the conquerors were before their eyes at the very moment: "Your country is desolate, your cities are burned with fire: your land, strangers devour it in your presence, and it is desolate, as overthrown by strangers." (Isa. 1:7.)

Another vivid image of Israel's contamination by sin is: "Thy silver is become dross, thy wine mixed with water." (Isa. 1:22.) Intermingled with such images — all, impressively, from a single chapter — comes a scenario for righteousness, again vivid and specific so that a sinner drawn toward repentance would know exactly what he or she should do:

> Learn to do well; seek judgment, relieve the oppressed, judge the fatherless, plead for the widow.
>
> Come now, and let us reason together, saith the Lord: though your sins be as scarlet, they shall be as white as snow; though they be red like crimson, they shall be as wool. (Isa. 1:17-18.)

Amos, a shepherd-prophet who preceded Isaiah on the same mission, paints an equally vivid picture of Israel's sins:

> Woe to them that are at ease in Zion, and trust in the mountain of Samaria, which are named chief of the nations, to whom the house of Israel came! . . .
>
> That lie upon beds of ivory, and stretch themselves upon their couches, and eat the lambs out of the flock, and the calves out of the midst of the stall;
>
> That chant to the sound of the viol, and invent to themselves instruments of musick, like David;
>
> That drink wine in bowls, and anoint themselves with the chief ointments: but they are not grieved for the affliction of Joseph. (Amos 6:1, 4-6.)

Surely, to a desert people surrounded by enemies, the images of luxuriant security and protection in the twenty-third Psalm were endlessly comforting:

> The Lord is my shepherd; I shall not want.
>
> He maketh me to lie down in green pastures: he leadeth me beside the still waters.
>
> He restoreth my soul: he leadeth me in the paths of righteousness for his name's sake.
>
> Yea, though I walk through the valley of the shadow of

17

death, I will fear no evil: for thou art with me; thy rod and thy staff they comfort me.

Thou preparest a table before me in the presence of mine enemies: thou anointest my head with oil; my cup runneth over.

Surely goodness and mercy shall follow me all the days of my life: and I will dwell in the house of the Lord for ever.

PARALLEL STRUCTURE

Hebrew poetry, which comprises much of the text of the Old Testament, exhibits several subtle forms of parallelism; but one of the most effective to me is synonymous parallelism. Instead of saying a thought once and then developing details of that idea, an Old Testament writer would frequently recast the thought twice or even oftener in different words. The effect is to engage the mind in a series of images that produce their own mood, tone, and direction instead of relying on the power of logic. To my way of thinking, this single device is extremely effective in allowing the reader to feel and absorb the thought and to perceive it in beauty. Here are some examples of synonymous parallelism:

Who shall ascend into the hill of the Lord? or who shall stand in his holy place? (Ps. 24:3.)

Shew me thy ways, O Lord; teach me thy paths. (Ps. 25:4.)

Examine me, O Lord, and prove me; try my reins and my heart. (Ps. 26:2.)

The Lord is my light and my salvation; whom shall I fear? the Lord is the strength of my life; of whom shall I be afraid? (Ps. 27:1.)

Ah sinful nation, a people laden with iniquity, a seed of evildoers, children that are corrupters: they have forsaken the Lord, they have provoked the Holy One of Israel unto anger, they are gone away backward.

Why should ye be stricken any more? ye will revolt more and more: the whole head is sick, and the whole heart faint.

From the sole of the foot even unto the head there is no

soundness in it; but wounds, and bruises, and putrifying sores: they have not been closed, neither bound up, neither mollified with ointment. . . .

Your new moons and your appointed feasts my soul hateth: they are a trouble unto me; I am weary to bear them. . . .

Wash you, make you clean; put away the evil of your doings from before mine eyes; cease to do evil. (Isa. 1:4-6, 16-17.)

The following long poetic passage from Job bears quotation simply for the versatility and subtlety of its parallelism:

> After this opened Job his mouth, and cursed his day.
> And Job spake, and said,
> Let the day perish wherein I was born, and the night in which it was said, There is a man child conceived.
> Let that day be darkness; let not God regard it from above, neither let the light shine upon it.
> Let darkness and the shadow of death stain it; let a cloud dwell upon it; let the blackness of the day terrify it.
> As for that night, let darkness seize upon it; let it not be joined unto the days of the year, let it not come into the number of the months.
> Lo, let that night be solitary, let no joyful voice come therein.
> Let the stars of the twilight thereof be dark; let it look for light, but have none; neither let it see the dawning of the day:
> Why died I not from the womb? why did I not give up the ghost when I came out of the belly?
> For now should I have lain still and been quiet, I should have slept: then had I been at rest. (Job 3:1-7, 9, 11, 13.)
> Shall mortal man be more just than God? shall a man be more pure than his maker? (Job 4:17.)
> Behold, happy is the man whom God correcteth: therefore despise not thou the chastening of the Almighty:
> For he maketh sore and bindeth up: he woundeth, and his hands make whole. (Job 5:17-18.)

19

DIVERSITY OF FORMS

The Old Testament is a large book, three times the size of the New Testament and twice as large as the Book of Mormon. Many hands writing in many different epochs have produced it, and these diversities of personality and emphases are paralleled by the diversity of forms. There are prose and poetry in rich abundance, a dramatic debate in Job, oratory in Deuteronomy, the epic stories of Abraham and Joseph, narrations and history, Nathan's parable, hymns of praise, proverbs, the lyrical story of Ruth, and fascinating psychological "short stories" featuring the all-too-human characteristics of men like Samson and David. In its variety of literary forms, the Old Testament is the richest scripture.

In short, although the Old Testament deserves our attention for its religious contributions — the subject that will occupy the remainder of this volume — it is equally deserving for its literary contributions to our culture.

Part II

OLD TESTAMENT
CONCEPTS OF GOD

Chapter 4
"I AM THAT I AM"

The Old Testament embodies the most fundamental ideas about God available in our Judeo-Christian culture. From it, even before the process of canonization began but certainly since then, have come affirmations of his existence, his creative role in nature and in human history, his revelations to his prophets, his concern for human beings, his universal influence, and his divine sovereignty. These are all meaningful functions and attributes of Deity.

But surely undergirding all of these concepts is the faith of Old Testament writers that God exists — that he is a living, personal, ethical being who can and does communicate with human beings. He is a God who gives people a sense of security, purpose, and meaning about their lives, thus satisfying their religious needs and aspirations.

From beginning to end, Old Testament writers affirm God's existence in a variety of ways. Let me share with you five of my favorite testimonies of God from the Old Testament.

A PERSONAL VISITATION TO MOSES

In this first example from Exodus 3:1-14, God reveals himself in a mysterious, even terrifying way—through the bush that burns without being consumed. He calls Moses to a compelling mission and speaks his name in one of the most awesome scenes ever recorded.

As Moses tends the flock of his father-in-law, Jethro, the priest of Midian, he follows them in their wanderings to a portion of the desert near Mount Horeb. It is unclear whether Horeb had this name even before Moses' experience or whether it became known by that name after Moses returned with his message.

And the angel of the Lord appeared unto him in a flame of fire out of the midst of a bush: and he looked, and, behold, the bush burned with fire, and the bush was not consumed. . . .

And when the Lord saw that he turned aside to see, God called unto him out of the midst of the bush, and said, Moses, Moses. And he said, Here am I.

And he said, Draw not nigh hither: put off thy shoes from off thy feet, for the place whereon thou standest is holy ground.

Moreover he said, I am the God of thy father, the God of Abraham, the God of Isaac, and the God of Jacob. And Moses hid his face; for he was afraid to look upon God.

And the Lord said, I have surely seen the affliction of my people which are in Egypt, and have heard their cry by reason of their taskmasters; for I know their sorrows;

And I am come down to deliver them out of the hand of the Egyptians, and to bring them up out of that land unto a good land and a large, unto a land flowing with milk and honey; unto the place of the Canaanites, and the Hittites, and the Amorites, and the Perizzites, and the Hivites, and Jebusites.

Now therefore, behold, the cry of the children of Israel is come unto me: and I have also seen the oppression wherewith the Egyptians oppress them.

Come now therefore, and I will send thee unto Pharaoh,

that thou mayest bring forth my people the children of Israel out of Egypt.

Overcome and filled with trepidation, Moses responded, "Who am I, that I should go unto Pharaoh, and that I should bring forth the children of Israel out of Egypt?" God, responding directly to Moses' unvoiced fears, reassured him, "Certainly I will be with thee; and this shall be a token unto thee, that I have sent thee: When thou hast brought forth the people out of Egypt, ye shall serve God upon this mountain."

Then Moses asked the great question that human beings have addressed to God in one form or another since the beginning of the world:

> Behold, when I come unto the children of Israel, and shall say unto them, The God of your fathers hath sent me unto you; and they shall say to me, What is his name? what shall I say unto them?
>
> And God said unto Moses, I AM THAT I AM: and he said, Thus shalt thou say unto the children of Israel, I AM hath sent me unto you.

THE INTIMATE TRUST OF THE PSALMIST

In a spirit of trust and rejoicing, the Psalmist provides my second example. He exultantly affirms the presence of God throughout the world in a succession of images that contrast the immensity of the universe with the intimacy of God's care:

> Whither shall I go from thy spirit? or whither shall I flee from thy presence?
>
> If I ascend up into heaven, thou art there: if I make my bed in hell, behold, thou art there.
>
> If I take the wings of the morning, and dwell in the uttermost parts of the sea;
>
> Even there shall thy hand lead me, and thy right hand shall hold me.
>
> If I say, Surely the darkness shall cover me; even the night shall be light around me.

25

> Yea, the darkness hideth not from thee; but the night shineth as the day: the darkness and the light are both alike to thee. (Ps. 139:7-12.)

PROVERBS' VIEW OF WISDOM

The author of Proverbs affirms God as the unfailing fountainhead of wisdom, urging his hearers to rely on a close personal relationship with God as the most constant factor in an uncertain world:

> Trust in the Lord with all thine heart; and lean not unto thine own understanding.
> In all thy ways acknowledge him, and he shall direct thy paths.
> Be not wise in thine own eyes: fear the Lord, and depart from evil.
> It shall be health to thy navel, and marrow to thy bones. (Prov. 3:5-8.)

ELIJAH'S DRAMATIC CONTEST

The prophet Elijah is one of the most colorful and dramatic witnesses for God in the Old Testament. His fervent and unwavering belief in the existence of God stands in sharp contrast to the fickleness of the Israelites, eager to be enticed into worshipping the false gods of neighboring tribes. In Elijah's day, Israel's king, Ahab, had married Jezebel, a Phoenician, who had brought with her a retinue of priests of Baal. Their activities were financed by the taxes of the Israelites whose faith they sought to undermine.

In a flamboyant public confrontation recorded in 1 Kings 18, Elijah challenged Ahab, "Now therefore send, and gather to me all Israel unto mount Carmel, and the prophets of Baal four hundred and fifty, and the prophets of the groves four hundred, which eat at Jezebel's table."

Ahab accepted the challenge and collected the people and priests. The biblical account does not record the number present on that occasion, and surely it is not realistic to suppose that the entire population of the nation was in attendance. Certainly, however, a sizeable number of people who were not counted among the 450 priests came to the gathering, for Elijah's opening statement is to them, "all the people": "How long halt ye between two opinions? if the Lord be God, follow him: but if Baal, then follow him." The people, probably not only skeptical but also cautious about incurring the king's displeasure, "answered him not a word."

Rather than laying a claim to popular support, Elijah underscored and intensified the numerical odds against him by reminding the people, "I, even I only, remain a prophet of the Lord; but Baal's prophets are four hundred and fifty men."

On such terms, how then could they refuse any reasonable contest of power that he proposed? And, indeed, the terms that he laid down were eminently fair:

> Let them therefore give us two bullocks; and let them choose one bullock for themselves, and cut it in pieces, and lay it on wood, and put no fire under: and I will dress the other bullock, and lay it on wood, and put no fire under:
>
> And call ye on the name of your gods, and I will call on the name of the Lord: and the God that answereth by fire, let him be God. And all the people answered and said, It is well spoken.
>
> And Elijah said unto the priests of Baal, Choose you one bullock for yourselves, and dress it first; for ye are many; and call on the name of your gods, but put no fire under.
>
> And they took the bullock which was given them, and they dressed it, and called on the name of Baal from morning even unto noon, saying, O Baal, hear us. But there was no voice, nor any that answered. And they leaped upon the altar which was made.
>
> And it came to pass at noon, that Elijah mocked them, and said, Cry aloud: for he is a god; either he is talking, or he is pursuing, or he is in a journey, or peradventure he sleepeth, and must be awaked.
>
> And they cried aloud, and cut themselves after their man-

27

ner with knives and lancets, till the blood gushed out upon them.

This spectacle continued until "the time of the offering of the evening sacrifice," attesting at least to the patience of the people and to the faith, however misplaced, of the priests of Baal. Then Elijah intervened sharply by calling the people to gather around him and the broken altar of Jehovah. With twelve stones, one for each of the twelve sons of Jacob, he repaired the altar and made a trench around it "as great as would contain two measures of seed." After arranging the wood and the pieces of slaughtered bull on top of the altar, he then asked for four barrels of water to be poured over the sacrifice and the wood. It is not clear from the record who performed this labor, whether he had some assistants who still believed in the God of Israel or whether the people themselves, fully convinced of the impotence of Baal, willingly fetched the water. In any case, Elijah had the sacrifice drenched not once but three times, filling the trench.

Then, in the dramatic dusk,

> Elijah the prophet came near, and said, Lord God of Abraham, Isaac, and of Israel, let it be known this day that thou art God in Israel, and that I am thy servant, and that I have done all these things at thy word.
>
> Hear me, O Lord, hear me, that this people may know that thou art the Lord God, and that thou hast turned their heart back again.
>
> Then the fire of the Lord fell, and consumed the burnt sacrifice, and the wood, and the stones, and the dust, and licked up the water that was in the trench.
>
> And when all the people saw it, they fell on their faces: and they said, The Lord, he is the God; the Lord, he is the God.

Sarcastic and sharp before the priests of Baal, Elijah is humble and self-effacing before Jehovah.

ISAIAH'S WITNESS OF A LIVING GOD

Like Elijah, all of the great writing prophets declare with authority and assurance that they are spokesmen for a living God. To read Amos, Hosea, Micah, Isaiah, Jeremiah, and Ezekiel is to be in the presence of men who have experienced God, not as an abstract ideal or as an ethical principle, but as a vital and unmediated reality. Isaiah's vision of God upon his throne, the vision that confirmed him as a prophet, illustrated his conviction:

> In the year that king Uzziah died I saw also the Lord sitting upon a throne, high and lifted up, and his train filled the temple.
>
> Above it stood the seraphims: each one had six wings; with twain he covered his face, and with twain he covered his feet, and with twain he did fly.
>
> And one cried unto another, and said, Holy, holy, holy, is the Lord of hosts: the whole earth is full of his glory.
>
> And the posts of the door moved at the voice of him that cried, and the house was filled with smoke.
>
> Then said I, Woe is me! for I am undone; because I am a man of unclean lips, and I dwell in the midst of a people of unclean lips: for mine eyes have seen the King, the Lord of hosts.
>
> Then flew one of the seraphims unto me, having a live coal in his hand, which he had taken with the tongs from off the altar:
>
> And he laid it upon my mouth, and said, Lo, this hath touched thy lips; and thine iniquity is taken away, and thy sin purged.
>
> Also I heard the voice of the Lord, saying, Whom shall I send, and who will go for us? Then said I, Here am I; send me. (Isa. 6:1-8.)

CONCLUSION

It is neither possible nor necessary for us to know all we wish to know about God. There is great value in living

29

by faith. What is vital to our life as religious persons is to believe that he exists. Our faith in his existence is the foundation of our faith that righteousness and goodness will ultimately triumph. If God exists, the things we cherish most — truth, love, beauty, goodness, integrity, and freedom — are not ultimately at the mercy of any unscrupulous individual, the hazards of mortality, or the menace of nuclear holocaust. Faith in the existence of a personal, divine being means also a faith in the eternal life of human beings. If personality is in command in the universe, human personality can be preserved.

Even if God did not exist, our human life would be rich with good and loving things; but those things would be overshadowed by the ultimate futility that would come with the inevitable end of life. The Old Testament is reassuring about God's existence and about the purposefulness of human experience. It affirms God's nature and being as one that thoughtful, sensitive human beings can worship with confidence and with fervor. It is those attributes, as revealed by the Old Testament, that succeeding chapters will explore.

Chapter 5

GOD THE REVELATOR

The Old Testament can be described as a sustained narrative of God's revelation of himself and his will over and over again to his prophets. These prophets have a dual purpose. Not only do they receive God's revelation of himself to them—which makes them prophets—but they also receive his will for his people. Among the most precious words in the Old Testament are those moments of contact between God and these individuals, in which a man becomes a prophet.

Genesis 12:1-3 describes the beginning of the house of Israel when God called Abram (Abraham) to leave his native country and to establish a new nation, a people destined to be a blessing to humankind, in a country God promised him:

> Now the Lord had said unto Abram, get thee out of thy country, and from thy kindred, and from thy father's house, unto a land that I will shew thee:
>
> And I will make of thee a great nation, and I will bless thee, and make thy name great; and thou shalt be a blessing:
>
> And I will bless them that bless thee, and curse him that curseth thee: and in thee shall all families of the earth be blessed.

31

Abraham's feelings and first response to this commandment are not recorded, but his obedience is.

Moses, who received the revelation of God in the burning bush, resisted the prophetic call. It is oddly endearing to think of someone with the stature of Moses demurring out of fear of others or of his own inadequacies: "Behold, they will not believe me, nor hearken unto my voice: for they will say, The Lord hath not appeared unto thee. . . . O my Lord, I am not eloquent, neither heretofore, nor since thou hast spoken unto thy servant: but I am slow of speech, and of a slow tongue." (Ex. 4:1, 10-11.) In light of Moses' public actions from that point on, such hesitancy seems to reveal the magnitude of Moses' faith.

The writing prophets—Amos, Hosea, Micah, Isaiah, Jeremiah, and Ezekiel—all spoke for God in the first person. Amos, a prophet from the kingdom of Judah, went north to Bethel, a sacred shrine in Israel, and spoke the mind of God to the Israelites. Amaziah, the high priest, angrily told Amos: "O thou seer, go, flee thee away into the land of Judah, and there eat bread, and prophesy there: But prophesy not again any more at Beth-el: for it is the king's chapel, and it is the king's court."

Amos responded by declaring his call—his credentials, if you will—in two verses that breathe both conviction and humility:"I was no prophet, neither was I a prophet's son; but I was an herdsman, and a gatherer of sycomore fruit: And the Lord took me as I followed the flock, and the Lord said unto me, Go, prophesy unto my people Israel." (Amos 7:14-15.)

Micah also expressed confidence in his divine commission: "But truly I am full of power by the spirit of the Lord, and of judgment, and of might, to declare unto Jacob his transgression, and to Israel his sin." (Micah 3:8.)

Jeremiah gives us a few more details of his own proph-

etic calling—again a pattern of resistance, then acceptance:

> Then the word of the Lord came unto me, saying,
> Before I formed thee in the belly I knew thee; and before
> thou camest forth out of the womb I sanctified thee, and I
> ordained thee a prophet unto the nations.
> Then said I, Ah, Lord God! Behold, I cannot speak: for
> I am a child.
> But the Lord said unto me, Say not, I am a child: for
> thou shalt go to all that I shall send thee, and whatsoever I
> command thee thou shalt speak.
> Be not afraid of their faces: for I am with thee to deliver
> thee, saith the Lord.
> Then the Lord put forth his hand, and touched my mouth.
> And the Lord said unto me, Behold, I have put my words in
> thy mouth.
> See, I have this day set thee over the nations and over
> the kingdoms, to root out, and to pull down, and to destroy,
> and to throw down, to build, and to plant. (Jer. 1:4-10.)

Jeremiah's writings have preserved for us the sensitivity of a personality who suffered from the rejection of
his people and the burden of his calling.

The Old Testament introduced to the world a new
kind of prophet. History provides two models of equally
great religious leaders: exemplars and emissaries. In India
and China, Lao-tze, Confucius, Buddha, and many
nameless Hindu gurus won adherents by their exemplary
lives. They faced the dilemmas of mortal life and suffering with wisdom, found solutions, developed inter-
pretations, and expounded them in memorable ways.
Some, particularly the Hindus and Lao-tze, believed in
God but claimed no revelation from him. I believe that
they were inspired of God in their ethical insights, but
they did not claim God's authority as they preached and
taught. In my view, they were the "angels" to their nation
that Alma longed to be in a stirring Book of Mormon
passage; after he expressed his wish, he realized that the

Lord was already meeting that need in His own way. Acknowledging that the Lord granted all people "their desire," whether "unto salvation or unto destruction," Alma expressed his understanding of how the Lord accomplished that end in a way that was comprehensible and just and that respected the free choice of those individuals:

> Now, seeing that I know these things, why should I desire more than to perform the work which I have been called?
>
> Why should I desire that I were an angel, that I could speak unto the ends of the earth?
>
> For behold, the Lord doth grant unto all nations, of their own nation and tongue, to teach his word, yea, in wisdom, all that he seeth fit that they should have; therefore we see that the Lord doth counsel in wisdom, according to that which is just and true. (Alma 29:6-8.)

The exemplary leaders I have mentioned were certainly teaching "their own nation and tongue" in ways acceptable to their culture. It is impressive to me that they were men who had mastered themselves and, to a great extent, their environment. They were intellectuals, reflective, meditative, serene, and clear in their thinking. Their teachings reflect these attributes.

How different were the Hebrew emissary prophets — Moses, Amos, Micah, Hosea, Isaiah, and Jeremiah. They spoke only because they believed that God had commanded them. They were sent. They made no pretense of being exemplary, and, in fact, their own record often stresses their inadequacies. They were listened to, not for the wisdom of their message, but because their hearers were convinced that the prophet spoke for God. And this belief seems to have been comparatively rare.

Emissary prophets were concerned with the present and future welfare of their people. They were emotional — angry, comforting, threatening, thundering like a force of nature and, like changes in nature, beautifully calm and serene after the storm. They have been called God-intoxicated men.

To the best of our knowledge, these emissary prophets appeared first in ancient Israel and are vividly portrayed in the Old Testament. They are the prototypes for such Christian leaders as Peter and Paul, who also spoke for Deity, and for Mohammed, who spoke for Allah.

In our own day, Joseph Smith continued the tradition of the emissary prophets who spoke for the Lord. Claiming no exemplary character, and being deeply involved in the daily struggles and survival of his people, he won adherents only when people, touched by his charisma or by the Holy Spirit, felt convinced that he spoke for God.

Hebrew prophets, the apostles of the Savior, and Joseph Smith were all exemplary in many ways, but this was not the basis of their appeal. They spoke in the name of God or Christ. None of them said. "Follow me. I have found the way to eternal life."

Jesus is the only great religious leader who spoke and acted both as an emissary and as an exemplar. In the emissary spirit, he said:

> I can of mine own self do nothing; as I hear, I judge: and my judgment is just; because I seek not mine own will, but the will of the Father which hath sent me. (John 5:30.)
> My doctrine is not mine, but his that sent me. If any man will do his will, he shall know of the doctrine, whether it be of God, or whether I speak of myself. (John 7:16-17.)

His exemplary role is illustrated throughout the Gospels. Perhaps the passage that stirs me most deeply is this one:

> I am the way, the truth, and the life: no man cometh unto the Father, but by me.
> If ye had known me, ye should have known my Father also. (John 14:6-7.)

35

Come unto me, all ye that labour and are heavy laden, and I will give you rest.

Take my yoke upon you, and learn of me; for I am meek and lowly in heart: and ye shall find rest unto your souls. (Matt. 11:28-29.)

Chapter 6

GOD THE CREATOR

One of the most powerful messages of the Old Testament is announced in its opening words: "In the beginning God created the heaven and the earth." (Gen. 1:1.) Then in simple, dignified language, the sequence of creation is described. Two things are made immensely clear by the simple process of repetition: God created the world, and those creations were good, serving his purposes.

Thus, two of the most important concepts the Old Testament teaches about God are that creativity is a fundamental part of his personality and that the earliest act he is recorded as performing was a creative one.

The Old Testament does not tell us much about the process or the techniques of creation. God simply said, "Let there be light: and there was light." (Gen. 1:3.) We make a big mistake, in my opinion, by trying to make a scientific account out of the biblical story. It is important to remember that it was written in a prescientific age by people whose purpose was a religious one—to glorify God, not to explain his works.

I believe that we can glorify God with the works of our intellects and that understanding God allows us to worship him more fully. However, I also firmly believe that we should not wrest texts into purposes other than those for which they were designed. In the Old Testament, we must accept God working in his vast dominions with his supernal knowledge. Isaiah, speaking for the Creator, gives us the right perspective:

> For my thoughts are not your thoughts, neither are your ways my ways, saith the Lord.
> For as the heavens are higher than the earth, so are my ways higher than your ways, and my thoughts than your thoughts. (Isa. 55:8-9.)

It seems much more important to me to accept the Hebrew perspective of a purposeful world that reflects the creative will and power of God, a world designed with human beings in mind and who came into being by that same divine will to create. Such a perspective is radically different from one that sees the world as a random or capricious production by competing gods, as is common in many mythologies, or even as the reasonable and predictable result of scientific laws and processes, certainly awesome but also chillingly impersonal and uncaring.

In contrast, sense the rejoicing in creation apparent in these verses from the Psalms and from Isaiah.

> The heavens declare the glory of God; and the firmament sheweth his handywork.
> Day unto day uttereth speech, and night unto night sheweth knowledge. (Ps. 19:1-2.)
> The earth is the Lord's, and the fulness thereof; the world, and they that dwell therein.
> For he hath founded it upon the seas, and established it upon the floods. (Ps. 24:1-2).
> For the Lord is a great God, and a great King above all gods.
> In his hand are the deep places of the earth: the strength of the hills is his also.

The sea is his, and he made it: and his hands formed the dry land.

O come, let us worship and bow down: let us kneel before the Lord our maker.

For he is our God; and we are the people of his pasture, and the sheep of his hand. To day if ye will hear his voice,

Harden not your heart, as in the provocation, and as in the day of temptation in the wilderness:

When your fathers tempted me, and saw my work. (Ps. 95:3-9.)

I have made the earth, and created man upon it: I, even my hands, have stretched out the heavens, and all their host have I commanded. (Isa. 45:12.)

Hearken unto me, O Jacob and Israel, my called; I am he; I am the first, I also am the last.

Mine hand also hath laid the foundation of the earth, and my right hand hath spanned the heavens: when I call unto them, they stand up together. (Isa. 48:12-13.)

Who is not moved by the sheer exultation in God's power and overwhelming personal role in creation that the Old Testament so vividly witnesses?

In general, three philosophies define God by a relationship to his creations, including human beings.

The first philosophy, pantheism, identifies the Creator with all that is. God is in the mountains and the rivers, and God is the mountains and rivers. Although we are most accustomed to it today in the form of transcendentalism, a philosophy worked out by the American philosopher and writer Ralph Waldo Emerson, pantheism's roots run to the oldest of all nonrevealed religions. Probably it is an outgrowth of the paganism that deified the forces of nature and made gods of the thunder and rain. In pantheism, of course, Jesus Christ would simply be an extraordinary individual who was able to concentrate the God-essence that is in everything and everyone to an unusual extent and express it in a very remarkable way.

In contrast, the second philosophy, deism, developed during the Enlightenment of the seventeenth and eighteenth centuries, when rationality and logic assumed great importance in western thought. The deist's position is that God is the clock-maker. He created nature and human beings, then left them to perform the functions for which he created them, observing but not interfering, performing miracles, or answering prayers. In a strict deistic view, Jesus Christ's claims of atonement and resurrection would have to be considered in one of two ways: either they were part of the "mechanism" built into the clock of human history since the beginning and hence inevitable—without his free choice—or else his claims of being God are overstated and he should be regarded as a good man whose life and personal example are an inspiration to others.

The third philosophy is theism. According to this view, God is a person and a personality, not just a force. He is continuously active in nature and human affairs, but he is not in them. His creative work has no end, but he has a separate identity, separate powers, and separate interests. Theism thus combines some of the elements of pantheism and deism by being both immanent (immediately concerned with human beings and the world in which we live) and transcendant (above and separate from human beings and our world).

The Old Testament depicts God in theistic terms as a personal being, apart from nature, the master of nature, but acting through nature:

> The Lord by wisdom hath founded the earth; by understanding hath he established the heavens.
> By his knowledge the depths are broken up, and the clouds drop down the dew.
> My son, let not them depart from thine eyes: keep sound wisdom and discretion:
> So shall they be life unto thy soul, and grace to thy neck.

40

Then shalt thou walk in thy way safely, and thy foot shall not stumble.

When thou liest down, thou shalt not be afraid: yea, thou shalt lie down, and thy sleep shall be sweet.

Be not afraid of sudden fear, neither of the desolation of the wicked, when it cometh.

For the Lord shall be thy confidence, and shall keep thy foot from being taken. (Prov. 3:19-26.)

This God is concerned with people, with their behavior and their destiny. He is responsive to prayer, to persuasion. He suffers with his people.

One of the most profound and promising aspects of the creation story in the Old Testament is this remarkable statement: "So God created man in his own image, in the image of God created he him; male and female created he them." (Gen. 1:27.) How exhilarating to believe that human beings have partaken of the nature of God by being created in his image, and that like him they have the inborn capacity to create, to love, to be intelligent, to be free. Although our abilities are small compared to God's, we have his assurance that these divine attributes slumber within us, waiting to find expression.

To me, the hunger for creativity that is an ineradicable part of human nature is its own testimony to the creativity of God. Romain Rolland, a French novelist, expressed this concept with passionate eloquence:

Joy, furious joy, the sun that lights up all that is and will be, the God-like joy of creation. There is no joy but in creation. There are no living beings but those who create. All the rest are shadows hovering over the earth, strangers to life. All the joys of life are the joys of creation: love, genius, action— quickened by flames issuing from one and the same fire. . . . To create in the region of the body, or in the region of the mind, is to issue from the prison of the body; it is to ride upon the storm of life; it is to be He who is. To create is to

41

triumph over death. (*Jean Christophe* [New York: Modern Library, 1913], p.364.)

If we are in the image of our Creator, we too must be creative to fulfill our natures. We are not puppets or robots or sheep. We have hands, minds, imagination, and feelings that need to find expression. Only humans have hands capable of sustained, minute work. Only humans have elaborate languages and symbolic systems of thought. Great is our need to express our feelings and thoughts in ways that will relieve suffering and promote life and goodwill upon the earth. The Old Testament pushes us toward that creativity by giving us an image of God as a joyful, exultant creator, one who also created us in his image.

Chapter 7

GOD THE ETHICAL

When we contrast the Old Testament with Greek myths, the closest written records in time and space to come down to us, we see an immediate contrast in the nature of the deities each presents. The gods of Olympus are spiteful, jealous, capricious, vindictive, domineering, and exploitive. Certainly, many episodes recorded in the Old Testament might justly earn one or more of these adjectives as well; but as I read the Old Testament, I see the massacre of the Canaanites and the sacrifice of Jephthah's daughter as isolated incidents against a background of moral standards.

God is ethical in his relations to human beings and unrelenting in his requirements that human beings be ethical with each other. The message of the writing prophets—Amos, Hosea, Micah, Isaiah, Jeremiah, and Ezekiel—is unmistakable. Flattery, offerings, bribes, and praises are not part of the worship of Israel's god. On the contrary, not even praise and sacrifice are meritorious unless accompanied by moral relations with one's fellow human beings.

Moses, speaking for God, said: "Ye shall be holy; for I the Lord your God am holy." (Lev. 29:2.) In the rest of that powerful and thought-provoking chapter, he defined holiness in terms of honesty, justice, and mercy in human relations.

Amos (760-740 B.C.) was the first of the writing prophets to declare the moral character of God. Speaking for God, Amos exclaimed:

> I hate, I despise your feast days, and I will not smell in your solemn assemblies.
>
> Though ye offer me burnt offerings, and your meat offerings, I will not accept them: neither will I regard the peace offerings of your fat beasts.
>
> Take thou away from me the noise of thy songs; for I will not hear the melody of thy viols.
>
> But let judgment run down as waters, and righteousness as a mighty stream. (Amos 5:21-24.)

And why is this worship rejected? Because in daily dealings with each other, these chosen people were unjust, deceitful, unfair, and oppressive to those least able to defend themselves:

> Woe to them that are at ease in Zion, and trust in the mountain of Samaria, which are named chief of the nations, to whom the house of Israel came! . . .
>
> That lie upon beds of ivory, and stretch themselves upon their couches, and eat the lambs out of the flock, and the calves out of the midst of the stall;
>
> That chant to the sound of the viol, and invent to themselves instruments of musick, like David;
>
> That drink wine in bowls, and anoint themselves with the chief ointments: but they are not grieved for the affliction of Joseph. (Amos 6:1, 4-6.)

The psalms recognize and praise the righteousness of the Lord, reciting a veritable litany of ethical qualities:

> Justice and judgment are the habitation of thy throne: mercy and truth shall go before thy face. (Ps. 89:14.)
>
> The Lord is upright: he is my rock, and there is no unrighteousness in him. (Ps. 92:15.)

For he cometh, for he cometh to judge the earth: he shall judge the world with righteousness, and the people with his truth. (Ps. 96:13.)

The Lord reigneth; let the earth rejoice; let the multitude of isles be glad thereof.

Clouds and darkness are round about him: righteousness and judgment are the habitation of his throne. (Ps. 97:1-2.)

His work is honourable and glorious: and his righteousness endureth for ever.

He hath made his wonderful works to be remembered: the Lord is gracious and full of compassion. . . .

The works of his hands are verity and judgment; all his commandments are sure.

They stand fast for ever and ever, and are done in truth and uprightness. (Ps. 111:3-4, 7-8.)

Blessed are the undefiled in the way, who walk in the law of the Lord.

Blessed are they that keep his testimonies, and that seek him with the whole heart.

They also do no iniquity: they walk in his ways.

Thou hast commanded us to keep thy precepts diligently.

O that my ways were directed to keep thy statutes!

Then shall I not be ashamed, when I have respect unto all thy commandments.

I will praise thee with uprightness of heart when I shall have learned thy righteous judgments.

I will keep thy statutes: O forsake me not utterly. (Ps. 119:1-8.)

Think of the cumulative effect on a people of bearing in their imaginations the image of an ethical and righteous God who required justice, obedience, truthfulness, honor, and compassion from his people. As generations passed, the "fear" of God capriciously punishing on a whim or for omitting a trifling part of the cult would disappear into a superstitious background, to be replaced by a relationship of truth in a God who needed to be feared only in the sense that rigorous standards and consistency of judgment always require appraisal of one's motives and behavior. Instead of being mysterious and alien, this is a God who is the model of righteous behavior for his people.

Isaiah, in eloquent language, describes God's rejection of Israel's religious ritual when keeping it has been used to justify neglecting the ethical life. How could a God of integrity and compassion accept praise from people who cheat their neighbors and take advantage of widows and orphans?

> To what purpose is the multitude of your sacrifices unto me? saith the Lord: I am full of the burnt offerings of rams, and the fat of fed beasts; and I delight not in the blood of bullocks, or of lambs, or of he goats.
> When ye come to appear before me, who hath required this at your hand, to treat my courts?
> Bring me no more vain oblations; incense is an abomination unto me; the new moons and sabbaths, the calling of assemblies, I cannot away with; it is iniquity, even the solemn meeting.
> Your new moons and your appointed feasts my soul hateth: they are a trouble unto me; I am weary to bear them.
> And when ye spread forth your hands, I will hide mine eyes from you: yea, when ye make many prayers, I will not hear: your hands are full of blood.
> Wash you, make you clean; put away the evil of your doings from before mine eyes; cease to do evil;
> Learn to do well; seek judgment, relieve the oppressed, judge the fatherless, plead for the widow.
> Come now, and let us reason together, saith the Lord: though your sins be as scarlet, they shall be as white as snow; though they be red like crimson, they shall be as wool. (Isa. 1:11-18.)

Micah speaks eloquently of the kind of religious offering acceptable to an ethical God:

> Wherewith shall I come before the Lord, and bow myself before the high God? shall I come before him with burnt offerings, with calves of a year old?

46

> Will the Lord be pleased with thousands of rams, or with
> ten thousands of rivers of oil? shall I give my firstborn for
> my transgression, the fruit of my body for the sin of my soul?
> He hath shewed thee, O man, what is good; and what
> doth the Lord require of thee, but to do justly, and to love
> mercy, and to walk humbly with thy God? (Micah 6:6-8.)

It is important to remember that ethics are not the same as religion. There are many aspects of the religious life and several legitimate ways to be religious, either individually or in a congregation. One aspect is intellectual: a knowledge of theology, scripture, and religious history is valuable. Ritual, church activity, and attending services bind an individual to his or her cobelievers. Christian service and personal worship of God through prayer are also essential to the religious life.

The unique and powerful emphasis in the Old Testament is the repeated declaration of God through his prophet-spokesmen that none of these ways of expressing religious values are acceptable to him unless they are accompanied by justice and mercy in our everyday relations with fellow human beings. In short, the Old Testament affirms that there can be no true spirituality without genuine social morality.

These ethical concepts are drawn directly from the nature of God himself. They constitute the core of the prophetic message of Elijah, Amos, Micah, Isaiah, and Jeremiah. They underlie the whole Mosaic law as spelled out in Deuteronomy. This concept is called ethical monotheism, Judaism's finest contribution to the world, in my opinion. God is ethical. And those who would serve him must also be ethical in their human relations.

Theology is of no value if it substitutes for social morality. Devils also believe and tremble. To be righteous, belief must include concern for our fellow human beings. Religious ordinances and rituals are vain if they do not encourage spirituality and morality. Church life is not an end in itself but a place to be inspired to go forth and deal honestly and compassionately with each other.

This is a lesson we must learn over and over. Reading the Hebrew prophets with their passionate clarity is, in my opinion, an excellent way to renew our commitment to justice and mercy.

Chapter 8

GOD THE JUST

Among the ethical elements in the character of God that we are enjoined to seek is the principle of justice. I have not made any kind of quantitative study of how often terms like judgment, justice, or just are applied to God in the Old Testament, but the very eloquence of the prophetic statements describing God's justice are of great interest.

Accustomed as we are to thinking of the Last Judgment in terms of our inevitable shortcomings, the obvious anticipation and confidence Hebrew writers manifest in the future judgments of God and their obvious love for God in his role as judge say more than possibly any other element about that relationship we call being a "chosen" people. Certainly they do not believe that they are excused from doing the works of righteousness. On the contrary, it is obvious that God holds them to a higher standard than their neighbors. But the candor and transparency they manifest toward God shows a level of faith and trust that makes us reappraise our own relationship with the Divine.

Read these exultant and eloquent expressions of the justice of God:

Thus saith the Lord, Let not the wise man glory in his wisdom, neither let the mighty man glory in his might, let not the rich man glory in his riches:

But let him that glorieth glory in this, that he understandeth and knoweth me, that I am the Lord which exercise lovingkindness, judgment, and righteousness, in the earth: for in these things I delight, saith the Lord. (Jer. 9:23-24.)

For I the Lord love judgment, I hate robbery for burnt offering; and I will direct their work in truth, and I will make an everlasting covenant with them. (Isa. 61:8.)

The Lord shall judge the people: judge me, O Lord, according to my righteousness, and according to mine integrity that is in me. (Ps. 7:8-9.)

For the word of the Lord is right; and all his works are done in truth.

He loveth righteousness and judgment: the earth is full of the goodness of the Lord. (Ps. 33:4-5.)

The Lord knoweth the days of the upright: and their inheritance shall be for ever. (Ps. 37:18.)

Because God is just, he requires justice in the lives of those who would serve him. Amos saw this clearly and declared it forcefully—a humble shepherd from the hills of Judea pronouncing judgment in Bethel, the shrine city of Israel. His scorching indictment of the rich who oppress the poor, thereby making mockery of their religious pretensions, is as relevant today as it was then, a permanent landmark on the road toward social justice:

They [the rich] hate him that rebuketh in the gate, and they abhor him that speaketh uprightly.

Forasmuch therefore as your treading is upon the poor, and ye take from him burdens of wheat: ye have built houses of hewn stone, but ye shall not dwell in them; ye have planted pleasant vineyards, but ye shall not drink wine of them.

For I know your manifold transgressions and your mighty sins: they afflict the just, they take a bribe, and they turn aside the poor in the gate from their right. . . .

Seek good, and not evil, that ye may live: and so the Lord, the God of hosts, shall be with you, as ye have spoken.

Hate the evil, and love the good, and establish judgment in the gate: it may be that the Lord God of hosts will be gracious unto the remnant of Joseph. (Amos 5:10-12, 14-15.)

Hear this, O ye that swallow up the needy, even to make the poor of the land to fail,

Saying, When will the new moon be gone, that we may sell corn? and the sabbath, that we may set forth wheat, making the ephah small, and the shekel great, and falsifying the balances by deceit?

That we may buy the poor for silver, and the needy for a pair of shoes; yea, and sell the refuse of the wheat?

The Lord hath sworn by the excellency of Jacob, Surely I will never forget any of their works. (Amos 8:4-7.)

The other prophets, in their own words, repeat the same message: that God demands righteousness from his people out of the depths of his own justice.

For the vineyard of the Lord of hosts is the house of Israel, and the men of Judah his pleasant plant: and he looked for judgment, but behold oppression; for righteousness, but behold a cry.

Woe unto them that join house to house, that lay field to field, till there be no place, that they may be placed alone in the midst of the earth! . . .

But the Lord of hosts shall be exalted in judgment, and God that is holy shall be sanctified in righteousness. . . .

Woe unto them that draw iniquity with cords of vanity, and sin as it were with a cart rope: . . . Woe unto them that call evil good, and good evil; that put darkness for light, and light for darkness; that put bitter for sweet, and sweet for bitter! . . .

Which justify the wicked for reward, and take away the righteousness of the righteous from him! (Isa. 5:7-8, 16, 18, 20, 23.)

The Lord will enter into judgment with the ancients of his people, and the princes thereof: for ye have eaten up the vineyard; the spoil of the poor is in your houses.

What mean ye that ye beat my people to pieces, and grind

the faces of the poor? saith the Lord God of hosts. (Isa. 3:14-15.)

Jeremiah's message is memorable in its denunciation of hypocrisy:

Thus saith the Lord of hosts, the God of Israel, Amend your ways and your doings, and I will cause you to dwell in this place. . . .

For if ye throughly amend your ways and your doings; if ye throughly execute judgment between a man and his neighbour;

If ye oppress not the stranger, the fatherless, and the widow, and shed not innocent blood in this place, neither walk after other gods to your hurt:

Then will I cause you to dwell in this place, in the land that I gave to your fathers, for ever and ever.

Behold, ye trust in lying words, that cannot profit.

Will ye steal, murder, and commit adultery, and swear falsely, and burn incense unto Baal, and walk after other gods whom ye know not;

And come and stand before me in this house, which is called by my name, and say, We are delivered to do all these abominations?

Is this house, which is called by my name, become a den of robbers in your eyes? Behold, even I have seen it, saith the Lord. (Jer. 7:1-11.)

The denunciations of the prophets were a reminder to the people that they stood convicted of violating the covenant made at Sinai and recorded in the books attributed to Moses. This covenant spells out not only correct principles but also correct practices:

Thou shalt not defraud thy neighbour, neither rob him: the wages of him that is hired shall not abide with thee all night until the morning. . . .

Ye shall do no unrighteousness in judgment, in meteyard, in weight, or in measure.

Just balances, just weights, a just ephah, and a just hin, shall ye have: I am the Lord your God, which brought you out of the land of Egypt.

Therefore shall ye observe all my statutes, and all my judgments, and do them: I am the Lord. (Lev. 19:13, 35-37.)

That which is altogether just shalt thou follow, that thou mayest live, and inherit the land which the Lord thy God giveth thee. (Deut. 16:20.)

Three of the Ten Commandments demand justice:

Thou shalt not steal.

Thou shalt not bear false witness against thy neighbour.

Thou shalt not covet thy neighbour's house, thou shalt not covet thy neighbour's wife, nor his manservant, nor his maidservant, nor his ox, nor his ass, nor any thing that is thy neighbour's. (Ex. 20:15-17.)

Nothing—neither piety, nor church activity, nor professions of faith—will substitute for honest dealings in human relations. This is the unequivocal message of the law of Moses and the prophets.

Chapter 9
GOD THE MERCIFUL

It is interesting to me that the ancient Hebrews rejoiced in the mercy of God and invoked it with the same
faith and confidence that they applied to his judgment.
Obviously, these two virtues were not seen as incom-
patible or contradictory in their thought.

The Lord's mercy is beautifully portrayed in Hosea,
whose marriage was a graphic example in miniature of
the Lord's relationship to Israel. His wife, Gomer, bore
him several children, then was unfaithful to him with
several lovers. At some point, she came to her senses
and returned to Hosea, who normally would have dis-
owned her. However, in love and mercy he received her
back and resumed the marriage.

Similarly, Israel deserted the Lord's law for the per-
missiveness of the cult of other gods. Hosea expresses
the Lord's anger and disappointment with backsiding
Israel:

> O Ephraim, what shall I do unto thee? O Judah, what
> shall I do unto thee? for your goodness is as a morning cloud,
> and as the early dew it goeth away. . . .
>
> For I desired mercy, and not sacrifice; and the knowledge
> of God more than burnt offerings.

But they like men have transgressed the covenant: there have they dealt treacherously against me. (Hosea 6:4, 6-7.)

My people are destroyed for lack of knowledge: because thou hast rejected knowledge, I will also reject thee, that thou shalt be no priest to me: seeing thou hast forgotten the law of thy God, I will also forget thy children. (Hosea 4:6.)

. For Israel slideth back as a backsliding heifer: now the Lord will feed them as a lamb in a large place. (Hosea 4:16.)

Hosea also spells out the method by which Israel can repent, meriting the Lord's mercy by doing mercifully.It is impressive to me that this call to repentance is not threatening or angry, but tender and pleading. The Lord reminds Israel of his love and promises them his mercy, appealing to them with gentleness and generosity:

Sow to yourselves in righteousness, reap in mercy; break up your fallow ground: for it is time to seek the Lord, till he come and rain righteousness upon you. (Hosea 10:12.)

Therefore turn thou to thy God: keep mercy and judgment, and wait on thy God continually. (Hosea 12:6.)

O Israel, return unto the Lord thy God; for thou hast fallen by thine iniquity.

Take with you words, and turn to the Lord: say unto him, Take away all iniquity, and receive us graciously: so will we render the calves of our lips.

Asshur shall not save us; we will not ride upon horses: neither will we say any more to the work of our hands, Ye are our gods: for in thee the fatherless findeth mercy.

I will heal their backsliding, I will love them freely: for mine anger is turned away from him.

I will be as the dew unto Israel: he shall grow as the lily, and cast forth his roots as Lebanon.

His branches shall spread, and his beauty shall be as the olive tree, and his smell as Lebanon.

They that dwell under his shadow shall return; they shall revive as the corn, and grow as the vine: the scent thereof shall be as the wine of Lebanon. (Hosea 14:1-7.)

No one could question the Lord's right to be angry and punitive, to set conditions of acceptance and probation. Instead, he appeals to Israel's memory of the loving, trusting faith that had existed between them and stands ready to heal the breach.

Just as God is merciful, so he requires us to be merciful, particularly to those who have no particular claim on us: the poor, the widow, the stranger, the fatherless, and the afflicted. In one of the most beautiful passages of all scripture, one that I have already cited, Micah describes true religion:

> Wherewith shall I come before the Lord, and bow myself before the high God? shall I come before him with burnt offerings, with calves of a year old?
>
> Will the Lord be pleased with thousands of rams, or with ten thousands of rivers of oil? shall I give my firstborn for my transgression, the fruit of my body for the sin of my soul?
>
> He hath shewed thee, O man, what is good; and *what doth the Lord require of thee, but to do justly, and to love mercy, and to walk humbly with thy God?* (Micah 6:6-8; italics added.)

Humility before God and person-to-person mercy result in spirituality and social morality. It would be difficult to make a case for removing them from any spiritual life.

The law of Moses mandates mercy:

> And when ye reap the harvest of your land, thou shalt not wholly reap the corners of thy field, neither shalt thou gather the gleanings of thy harvest.
>
> And thou shalt not glean thy vineyard, neither shalt thou gather every grape of thy vineyard; thou shalt leave them for the poor and stranger: I am the Lord your God. (Lev. 19: 9-10.)
>
> If there be among you a poor man of one of thy brethren within any of thy gates in thy land which the Lord thy God giveth thee, thou shalt not harden thine heart, nor shut thine hand from thy poor brother:
>
> But thou shalt open thine hand wide unto him, and shalt

57

surely lend him sufficient for his need, in that which he wanteth.

Beware that there be not a thought in thy wicked heart, saying, The seventh year, the year of release, is at hand; and thine eye be evil against thy poor brother, and thou givest him nought; and he cry unto the Lord against thee, and it be sin unto thee.

Thou shalt surely give him, and thine heart shall not be grieved when thou givest unto him: because that for this thing the Lord thy God shall bless thee in all thy works, and in all that thou puttest thine hand unto.

For the poor shall never cease out of the land: therefore I command thee, saying, Thou shalt open thine hand wide unto thy brother, to thy poor, and to thy needy, in thy land.

And if thy brother, an Hebrew man, or an Hebrew woman, be sold unto thee, and serve thee six years; then in the seventh year thou shalt let him go free from thee.

And when thou sendest him out free from thee, thou shalt not let him go away empty:

Thou shalt furnish him liberally out of thy flock, and out of thy floor, and out of thy winepress: of that wherewith the Lord thy God hath blessed thee thou shalt give unto him.

And thou shalt remember that thou wast a bondman in the land of Egypt, and the Lord thy God redeemed thee: therefore I command thee this thing to day. (Deut. 15:7-15.)

Thou shalt not oppress an hired servant that is poor and needy, whether he be of thy brethren, or of thy strangers that are in thy land within thy gates:

At his day thou shalt give him his hire, neither shall the sun go down upon it; for he is poor, and setteth his heart upon it: lest he cry against thee unto the Lord, and it be sin unto thee. . . .

Thou shalt not pervert the judgment of the stranger, nor of the fatherless; nor take a widow's raiment to pledge. (Deut. 24:14-15, 17.)

As we read these passages, the law of Moses seems to be describing the kinds of activities we would today term "charitable work." I find it particularly appropriate that the God of love defines mercy in terms of loving behavior. Beyond our baptism, confirmation, ordinations, prayers, and offerings to the Lord, he requires our mercy, compassion, love, and generosity to one another. We learn mercy by practicing the works of mercy.

This means that we visit the widows and others who are lonely, succor the disabled of mind and body, provide work for the unemployed, take an interest in children who need attention, and help people become more self-sufficient both at home and abroad. It means that we are troubled by the suffering of fellow human beings and do something to relieve it. It also means that our sharing is somewhat selfless in that we do not praise ourselves for these works or criticize others for needing our mercy. Nothing sours the sweetness of a loving act so quickly as the merest taint of self-congratulation on our generosity or sensitivity or tact!

It is not enough to pay a generous fast offering and leave compassionate service to the bishopric and Relief Society presidency. We must set aside time, energy, and means to help low-income and lonely people, the elderly, the disabled, and the alienated — all marginal members of our community, whether they be members of the Church or not.

I know a father of nine who seeks out one or two widows each month and works in their yards, or makes minor repairs on their homes. He has been doing this for several years. He is a true disciple of the prophets and of Jesus.

There are ways to show mercy that take neither time nor money, such as refraining from gossip, showing tolerance, not judging a neighbor, and forgiving offenses.

Chapter 10

GOD THE RATIONAL

In a beautiful passage in Proverbs 3:19-20, God is described as intelligence:

> The Lord by wisdom hath founded the earth; by understanding hath he established the heavens.
>
> By his knowledge the depths are broken up, and the clouds drop down the dew.

Wisdom, knowledge, understanding. For me, these qualities are inseparable from the power of God and his loving will to use that power on our behalf. His intelligence gives order to the universe and allows — even en-courages — us to devote part of our attention to rational analyses of the universe because an intelligent being brought it about.

Because of this rational perception of Deity, the Old Testament rejects irrational and superstitious attempts to explain life that were typical of Israel's ancient neighbors. An example is this memorable passage from Deuteronomy:

> When thou art come into the land which the Lord thy God giveth thee, thou shalt not learn to do after the abominations of those nations.

> There shall not be found among you any one that maketh his son or his daughter to pass through the fire, or that useth divination, or an observer of times, or an enchanter, or a witch,
>
> Or a charmer, or a consulter with familiar spirits, or a wizard, or a necromancer.
>
> For all that do these things are an abomination unto the Lord: and because of these abominations the Lord thy God doth drive them out from before thee.
>
> Thou shalt be perfect with the Lord thy God.
>
> For these nations, which thou shalt possess, hearkened unto observers of times, and unto diviners: but as for thee, the Lord thy God hath not suffered thee so to do. (Deut. 18: 9-14.)

Astrology, ouija boards, fortune-telling, spiritualism (seeking contact with the dead), and divination do not get us into contact with reality in a meaningful way. In place of irrational ways of dealing with life, the Israelites were admonished to obey the commandments, statutes, and laws of God, with the promise of prosperity and well being if they would. I love this expression of the dignity and majesty of law:

> Now these are the commandments, the statutes, and the judgments, which the Lord your God commanded to teach you, that ye might do them in the land whither ye go to possess it:
>
> That thou mightest fear the Lord thy God, to keep all his statutes and his commandments, which I command thee, thou, and thy son, and thy son's son, all the days of thy life; and that thy days may be prolonged.
>
> Hear therefore, O Israel, and observe to do it; that it may be well with thee, and that ye may increase mightily, as the Lord God of thy fathers hath promised thee, in the land that floweth with milk and honey.
>
> Hear, O Israel: The Lord our God is one Lord:
>
> And thou shalt love the Lord thy God with all thine heart, and with all thy soul, and with all thy might. (Deut. 6:1-5.)

When Jesus quoted this passage, he made a significant

addition: "Thou shalt love the Lord thy God with all thy heart, and with all thy soul, and *with all thy mind*." (Matt. 22:37; italics added.)

Obedience to law became the foundation of Israel's religion and has had far-reaching influence on human history. It would be difficult to exaggerate the role of law in our western and modern civilization. All science rests on the assumption that there are laws of nature—uniform ways in which the forces of nature act. These can be discovered, measured, observed, understood, and used by rational human beings. In our economic endeavors, in farming and manufacturing, we reckon with laws of our physical environment and obey them if we wish to achieve our goals.

The difference between a medicine man and a modern physician is likewise explained rationally. What a medicine man does to cure smallpox, for example, has little to do with the nature of the disease, whereas the doctor knows that it is caused by a germ and can be prevented by immunization.

In a democratic government, based on constitutional law, considerable rationality is made possible in civic life. The people are not at the mercy of dictatorial whims, but the system itself provides limits and checks upon the despotic tendencies of those whom it endows with power. Through the court system, people are judged not by individuals but by laws, even though the laws are interpreted by individuals. The rule of law asserts not only the primacy of legal procedures but also the concept that decisions must be reached in a rational and lawful manner. This is a tremendous step toward greater rationality and freedom in political and civic life. In such a society, social contract is based on the idea that reasonable people, reasoning together, will not need to have recourse to violence in an attempt to solve a problem.

One of the powerful messages of the passage cited

above is that we are to love God with our minds as well as our hearts, and that he is pleased with the respect accorded him by rational beings.

I believe that Old Testament writers, by emphasizing the importance of their obedience to law, have greatly influenced the economic, scientific, and political life of western civilization. It was natural and relatively easy for our forefathers, trained by their faith in the Bible to be obedient to God's laws, to learn obedience to the laws of nature and to constitutional law.

Certainly, in times of irrational and random violence that seem to characterize so much of our planet today, we need to affirm our faith in the processes of reasonable discourse, reaching deep for the faith that human beings can "reason together."

We must not forget the lesson learned from ancient Israel: that God is not capricious but instead is a rational, law-abiding being whose ways we can come to know and trust. From the prophets, we have learned to love the Lord with our minds as well as with our hearts. Religion is expressed with feeling and rests on faith, but it also includes rational elements. We need a knowledge of God's will and purpose to guide us in our expressions of faith and love. It is significant to me that the law itself includes this injunction to live in intimate knowledge of the law:

> And these words, which I command thee this day, shall be in thine heart:
> And thou shalt teach them diligently unto thy children, and shalt talk of them when thou sittest in thine house, and when thou walkest by the way, and when thou liest down, and when thou risest up.
> And thou shalt bind them for a sign upon thine hand, and they shall be as frontlets between thine eyes.
> And thou shalt write them upon the posts of thy house, and on thy gates.
> And thou shalt do that which is right and good in the sight of the Lord: that it may be well with thee. (Deut. 6: 6-9, 18.)

Chapter 11
GOD THE ONE

Ancient, primitive religions were polytheistic. They accepted a system of many gods, usually personifying forces of nature that affected human beings for good or ill. Polytheism sometimes developed into henotheism, a system in which one's own god is superior but in which less powerful gods also exist.

The Old Testament contains intimations of both polytheism and henotheism. Rachel took the "images," or household gods, of her father, Laban, when Jacob and his family returned to Canaan. (Gen. 31.) While the Israelites lived in Canaan, they experienced a constant struggle between loyalty to Jehovah and the seductions of the pagan gods of surrounding tribes.

It is to the credit of Moses and the writing prophets that Israel arrived at faith in one universal God — or monotheism. Its strongest expression is embodied in the Ten Commandments:

> Thou shalt have no other gods before me.
> Thou shalt not make unto thee any graven image, or any likeness of any thing that is in heaven above, or that is in the earth beneath, or that is in the water under the earth. (Ex. 20:3-4.)

However, God also asserts his incomparable primacy in other eloquent passages:

> Who hath measured the waters in the hollow of his hand, and meted out heaven with the span, and comprehended the dust of the earth in a measure, and weighed the mountains in scales, and the hills in a balance?
>
> Who hath directed the Spirit of the Lord, or being his counsellor hath taught him?
>
> With whom took he counsel, and who instructed him, and taught him in the path of judgment, and taught him knowledge, and shewed to him the way of understanding?
>
> Behold, the nations are as a drop of a bucket, and are counted as the small dust of the balance: behold, he taketh up the isles as a very little thing. (Isa. 40:12-15.)
>
> I am the Lord, and there is none else, there is no God beside me: I girded thee, though thou hast not known me:
>
> That they may know from the rising of the sun, and from the west, that there is none beside me. I am the Lord, and there is none else.
>
> I form the light, and create the darkness: I make peace, and create evil: I the Lord do all these things.
>
> Drop down, ye heavens, from above, and let the skies pour down righteousness: let the earth open, and let them bring forth salvation, and let righteousness spring up together; I the Lord have created it. (Isa. 45:5-8.)

This expansive and eloquent statement of monotheism is one of the powers of the Old Testament. Monotheism appeals to the rational mind that sees a need for unity in the universe and a master intelligence behind it. Monotheism also meets a person's religious need for loyalty not just to the superior, but to the supreme, an entity worthy of a commitment to veneration and service.

Believing in *one* God who is an ethical being of justice and mercy certainly implies that he is impartial—that all people are of equal value in his eyes. The Israelites were slow to learn this. They believed themselves specially favored of God above other peoples. It is possible to argue that the book of Jonah was written to correct this misconception.

The story of Jonah and the fish is so dramatic that many readers miss the religious message of the book. I once told the story of Jonah to a group of freshman medical students who squirmed all the way through it and insisted on arguing about the potential of human survival inside a fish. Whether he was or was not physically inside that fish does not affect the teachings of this book. As natural history, Jonah is a dubious source. Its value is the force and grace of its attack on ethnocentrism.

Jonah was called to preach repentance to the wicked gentile city of Nineveh. He fled in the opposite direction — to Tarshish. When the Lord renewed Jonah's mission in forceful terms, Jonah reluctantly but obediently went to Nineveh and preached repentance, threatening destruction if the people did not heed his warning. Jonah delivered his message grudgingly and anticipated the city's destruction. To his surprise and dismay, everyone in Nineveh from the king to the humblest citizen repented in sackcloth and ashes.

Jonah, meanwhile, had picked out a good vantage point on a hilltop, waiting for Nineveh's destruction, and was highly displeased with the humility of the people. God again taught his prophet a forcible lesson by preparing a gourd to shade Jonah. He later prepared a worm that destroyed the gourd, then asked pointedly, "Doest thou well to be angry for the gourd?" Jonah answered defiantly, "I do well to be angry, even unto death."

It is possible to read stinging rebuke softened by humor in God's response. It is also possible to read in it a standard of judgment that places an absolute value on human life — not Israelite life or life that obeys ritual requirements, but human life:

> Then said the Lord, Thou hast had pity on the gourd,

> for the which thou hast not laboured, neither madest it grow; which came up in a night, and perished in a night:
>
> And should not I spare Nineveh, that great city, wherein are more than sixscore thousand persons that cannot discern between their right hand and their left hand; and also much cattle? (Jonah 4:9-11.)

The fish incident is not the only aspect of the tale to question. As a so-called prophet, Jonah is a dubious character indeed. Imagine a prophet of God angry because the divine will is fulfilled! Imagine a prophet arguing with God over a gourd! And imagine every person in an entire city promptly and completely repenting! The book of Jonah appears to me, and to many others, to be not a historical account, but a parable created by a religious artist to teach a great idea that the people needed to understand—and to teach it in an interesting and delightful way.

The narrative of Jonah contains several ideas that the Jews needed to learn: (1) God is universal. The people of Nineveh are also his concern. (2) God is impartial. Even as Israel can repent and be saved, so can Nineveh. God's laws apply equally to all people. (3) God is merciful. His desire is to save, not destroy.

If God has these attributes, then we should have them too. Human beings have always been slow to realize that, beyond the differences of culture, talents, and capacities, we all have the same basic needs for food, shelter, health, respect, and acceptance. As persons, we are not to be judged as inferior or superior to one another. Each individual is sacred in the eyes of God and should be in ours. The book of Jonah is an effective attack on ethnocentrism.

Part III

OLD TESTAMENT CONTRIBUTIONS TO THE RELIGIOUS LIFE

Chapter 12
"NOT GOOD . . . TO BE ALONE"

The creation account in the first three chapters of Genesis has many challenging and interesting ideas in it. One that we have already discussed in Chapter 6 is: "So God created man in his own image, in the image of God created he him; male and female created he them." (Gen. 1:17.)

Just how God created man is not indicated, since the author either did not know the technical details or did not consider that aspect of creation important. The author does, however, supply additional details when it comes to the creation of the woman: Eve was purportedly made from a rib of Adam.

If taken literally as an account of a surgical operation, this narrative raises serious problems in a scientific age. In fact, Latter-day Saints do not take this story literally but are enjoined to regard it as figurative. However, if the ancient story is read as a human and religious description of the husband-wife relationship, it becomes remarkably instructive and valuable even in a modern age. Here again, the "how" of creation is not the concern of religion. Its purpose and value are. What can we learn from the creation of the first man and the first woman in Genesis?

The accounts in chapters 1 and 2 of Genesis seem to have combined two records that make several aspects of the creative process clear:

First, human beings are created in the image of God, as we have seen.

Second, Adam's body was created from the elements of the earth, although the process is not known: "And the Lord God formed man of the dust of the ground, and breathed into his nostrils the breath of life; and man became a living soul." (Gen. 2:7.)

Next, we see that creation was incomplete without a companion for Adam who would be fully worthy of his own divine origins: "And the Lord God said, It is not good that the man should be alone; I will make him an help meet for him." (Gen. 2:18.)

This third concept gives us an important message. Although Adam was the first human and did not have consciousness of himself as either alone or with someone, God knew that being alone was not good for a human being. "It is not good that the man should be alone." This statement is as profound as it is simple. It is a fundamental fact of life, verified by psychology, psychiatry, social work, and everyday human experience. After obtaining the physical necessities of life, a person's most pressing need is to be accepted, wanted, needed, and loved by one or more others — from infancy through old age.

After God observes that no one should be alone, he next creates "every beast of the field, and every fowl of the air; and brought them unto Adam to see what he would call them."

> And Adam gave names to all cattle, and to the fowl of the air, and to every beast of the field; but for Adam there was not found an help meet for him.
> And the Lord God caused a deep sleep to fall upon Adam,

and he slept: and he took one of his ribs, and closed up the flesh instead thereof;

And the rib, which the Lord God had taken from man, made he a woman, and brought her unto the man. (Gen. 2:19-22.)

Adam greets the woman with an expression of literal and metaphoric unity:

And Adam said, This is now bone of my bones, and flesh of my flesh: she shall be called Woman, because she was taken out of Man.

Therefore shall a man leave his father and his mother, and shall cleave unto his wife: and they shall be one flesh.

And they were both naked, the man and his wife, and were not ashamed. (Gen. 2:23-25.)

Life is social as well as individual. "We live, and move, and have our being" in each other as well as in God. (Acts 17:28.) It is profound that this fact should be recognized in the first mention of human creation.

A related idea is Adam's recognition that the woman is "bone of my bones, and flesh of my flesh," a person of the same nature with the same needs, belonging to the same kind. Marriages that are based on the differences between husband and wife, rather than their essential similarities, do violence to the very basis of human nature. I have always liked the additional symbolism that the rib is the bone closest to the heart and that it lacks virtually any other symbol than that of the heart: if it had been from the head or the foot, it could have implied superiority or inferiority; from the pelvis or thigh, mere sexual functioning; from the hand, a need to be grasped and held; or from the backbone, continual followership.

Another important message for marriage partners is Genesis 2:24: "Therefore shall a man leave his father and his mother, and shall cleave unto his wife." When a couple marry, their first loyalty is to each other. This means leaving home and living by themselves. I firmly believe that if they are not ready to be economically independent, they are not ready for marriage. This position contains no disrespect for in-laws. Couples can and should build and maintain fine family relationships, but undue dependence on one's extended family or being dominated by one's extended family is devastating to a tender, young relationship. Granted, the exact definition of these terms varies from culture to culture and family to family, but the principle is true universally.

The Old Testament consistently condemns promiscuity, infidelity, and adultery; but it accepts, celebrates, and even exalts marital sexuality as an important part of normal, God-approved relationships between husband and wife. Christianity has developed a concept of original sin derived from sexuality, but that belief is not present in the Old Testament. It is remarkable—and yet not at all astonishing—that the Old Testament's account of the creation of man and woman should contain so much that we still perceive as superlative good sense today.

The social emphasis in the Old Testament goes beyond personal life in the family. The law of Moses and the writings of the prophets spell out our social responsibility for the poor, the slave, the stranger, the widow, and the fatherless. Compassion is a commandment. One's duty to others is stressed much more emphatically than personal rights and privileges. The prophets were trying to save their nation; individuals within the nation will be saved as part of that collectivity.

Our modern western civilization has greatly stressed individualism. Democracy has encouraged it. Capitalism was inspired in part by Adam Smith's idea that if everyone sought his own interest, society as a whole would prosper. The Renaissance, the Enlightenment, and especially the Protestant Reformation broke away from the unifying dominance of the church and, in some instances, the state. Along with the immense power of this stress on individuality, we have also seen some of the problems that it creates, and I believe that the pendulum is swinging back to greater social consciousness.

Religion needs to recognize the value of both the individual and society. Human beings are individuals, and they also live together in society. The Hebrew prophets stressed that the well-being of the nation must be achieved through individual righteousness, and Ezekiel 18 is virtually a charter of individual responsibility for righteousness during the Babylonian captivity when there was no nation.

Latter-day Saints place a heavy emphasis on individual responsibility, growth, and salvation — on the righteous use of inalienable free agency. We also have an inspiring history of our efforts to create a Christian society. There is a great need to keep a balance by strengthening both the individual and society through our religious efforts.

The Old Testament was quite right when it stated: "It is not good that the man should be alone." We need one another. We need to think in social, as well as in individual, perspectives, both in the primary relationships of the family and in our human relationships in society.

Chapter 13

THE SABBATH: A BOON TO HUMAN BEINGS

When God established the Sabbath, its purpose was clear: the Sabbath was ordained to honor the Creator:

> Keep the sabbath day to sanctify it, as the Lord thy God hath commanded thee.
> Six days shalt thou labour, and do all thy work:
> But the seventh day is the sabbath of the Lord thy God. (Deut. 5:12-14.)

Honoring the Lord—remembering him, worshipping him, renewing and strengthening our faith in him, and viewing life again from an eternal perspective—is still the first purpose of this commandment. It is also a blessing to human beings in other ways, especially as a day of rest from hard labor and stressful obligations. Note the compassion, the universal and equal concern for everyone, including slaves, and also for the beasts:

> In it thou shalt not do any work, thou, nor thy son, nor thy daughter, nor thy manservant, nor thy maidservant, nor thine ox, nor thine ass, nor any of thy cattle, nor thy stranger

that is within thy gates; that thy manservant and thy maid-servant may rest as well as thou.

And remember that thou wast a servant in the land of Egypt, and that the Lord thy God brought thee out thence through a mighty hand and by a stretched out arm: therefore the Lord thy God commanded thee to keep the sabbath day. (Deut. 5:14-15.)

The Sabbath has been a joyful day to devout Jews throughout the centuries. Hasidic men still dance to wel-come the Sabbath, as though at a wedding. Mothers have special tablecloths and dishes for the Sabbath. A special ceremony of lighting the Sabbath candles makes each Sabbath a weekly event. In synagogue worship, the Sab-bath is a time of celebrating Israel's hopes for peace and restoration, a time for reading the law of Moses again and again, so that its principles will be fresh and beloved.

When I was fourteen, I worked on a ranch during the summer. Our day began at dawn. We had the cows milked, the pigs slopped, and the horses harnessed before breakfast at 7 A.M. We worked in the fields, pitching hay or digging postholes until 6:00 P.M. Then we did evening chores. This was our schedule six days a week. Sunday was a welcome day of rest.

One Sunday the boss asked us to round up a bunch of wild horses that were feeding on our alfalfa, robbing the ranch of needed hay for winter. We were in the saddle all day, either capturing or destroying the horses. I can still remember how long the next week seemed without that Sabbath day of rest behind us.

The forty-hour week with Saturday and Sunday free is a rather recent arrangement. Through the nineteenth century and into the twentieth, having Saturday after-noons free was considered liberal. For centuries, men, women, and children worked twelve and fourteen hours a day. In Jewish and Christian societies, the Sabbath was heaven-sent. Without it, slaves and laborers might have had to work day in and day out. Dr. Louis Zucker, late professor of biblical literature at the University of Utah, once told me that the Babylonians had a sabbath but it was not weekly and it was limited only to aristocrats. What other ancient cultures did to provide a day of rest I do not know. But I am grateful to Old Testament law for creating a day of rest, a time of worship for all people, and rest even for the beasts of the field.

Jesus added a wonderful concept to the purposes of the Sabbath. He recognized that the Sabbath should be appraised in human terms, as shown by the freedom he felt to heal and save life on the Sabbath:

> And it came to pass also on another sabbath, that he entered into the synagogue and taught: and there was a man whose right hand was withered.
>
> And the scribes and Pharisees watched him, whether he would heal on the sabbath day; that they might find an accusation against him.
>
> But he knew their thoughts, and said to the man which had the withered hand, Rise up, and stand forth in the midst. And he arose and stood forth.
>
> Then said Jesus unto them, I will ask you one thing; Is it lawful on the sabbath days to do good, or to do evil? to save life, or to destroy it?
>
> And looking round about upon them all, he said unto the man, Stretch forth thy hand. And he did so: and his hand was restored whole as the other. (Luke 6:6-10.)

The Sabbath is a day of rest, a time to remember the Lord. And there is no better way to honor the Lord than to bring healing, comfort, and blessings to his children as Jesus did.

In our urban, impersonal society, the Sabbath has become a day of recreation, a day to watch the Superbowl or World Series. For active Latter-day Saints, the Sabbath is often consumed in attending meetings, doing home teaching or visiting teaching, or holding family counseling sessions. Can we learn the deeper meaning of Sabbath observance by remembering its importance in Israel, enriched by the emphasis of Jesus? Can it be a time of spiritual growth to the individual and a day of reconciliation in our social relations?

We frequently ignore the need people have to know that someone cares about them. There are many elderly people, mostly women, who have neither spouses nor children and who sit alone in their homes day after day, night after night. They long to talk with someone.

The Sabbath is a golden opportunity to build good human relationships in the immediate family, in the extended family, in the neighborhood, and in the community. The Sabbath is not wholly fulfilled unless someone's burden has been eased or lifted.

Chapter 14
LIVE BY LAW

The Jewish word *Torah*, meaning the Law, is used in several ways. It is the name of the first five books of the Old Testament. It also refers to the specific moral and ritual commandments found in those five books. Furthermore, it can designate the principles of moral conduct contained within these books. It is in this last sense that we shall discuss it.

Lists of the laws are found in Exodus 20–23, Leviticus 19 and 25, and most completely in Deuteronomy 5–17. A very interesting story in 2 Kings 22:8-23 relates how the scroll of Deuteronomy was found in the temple and brought to the righteous king Josiah and the prophet Jeremiah. The king read it, was profoundly impressed, called his people together, had the book read to them, and had them vow to live by the laws contained therein. He then made a clean sweep of every figment of idolatrous worship in the temple and in the land. His own father, Manasseh, had introduced and encouraged such practices.

Scholars believe that Deuteronomy in its present form may have been written by prophets or followers of the prophets in the name of Moses and hidden in the temple to add authority to this highly prized Mosaic law. It is beautifully and forcefully written, whoever was the final author. Moses delivered this law as part of his farewell address to his people before they entered the land of Canaan.

In the first four chapters, Moses reviews all that the Lord has done to bring the Israelites to the land of Canaan. In chapters 5 through 27, he lays down the laws they are to observe in the land of Canaan. The concluding chapters, 28–34, are a promise and a curse on Israel, foretelling in graphic detail what will happen if the people obey or disobey the laws in the book. There is a foreboding that they will not obey and will be destroyed as a nation.

What are the strengths and limitations of the moral laws in Deuteronomy? What can modern Jews and Christians learn from these ancient standards of conduct?

First, these laws are specific, concrete, and detailed. They are not just correct principles but a list of correct behavior. Dr. Louis Zucker illustrated this by saying that he saw a student go through a heavy library door and let it close without looking to see if anyone were coming after him. The door struck another student on crutches who was following him. In ancient Israel there would have been a law: "When thou goest through a gate or door, thou shalt look behind thee to see if anyone is following close before thou lettest go of the gate or door." (I might add that this principle has been a law to me for some thirty years since I first heard of the incident.)

Note some examples of concreteness:

> Thou shalt not see thy brother's ox or his sheep go astray, and hide thyself from them: thou shalt in any case bring them again unto thy brother.
> And if thy brother be not nigh unto thee, or if thou know him not, then thou shalt bring it unto thine own house, and

it shall be with thee until thy brother seek after it, and thou shalt restore it to him again.

In like manner shalt thou do with his ass; and so shalt thou do with his raiment; and with all lost things of thy brother's, which he hath lost, and thou hast found, shalt thou do likewise: thou mayest not hide thyself.

Thou shalt not see thy brother's ass or his ox fall down by the way, and hide thyself from them: thou shalt surely help him to lift them up again. (Deut. 22:1-4.)

The ancient Israelites had a form of honeymoon leave, which not only had the practical effect of allowing a young couple to spend a great deal of time establishing a firm relationship, but which also had the practical effect of virtually guaranteeing conception so that, in case the husband were killed in battle, he would leave a descendant: "When a man hath taken a new wife, he shall not go out to war, neither shall he be charged with any business: but he shall be free at home one year, and shall cheer up his wife which he hath taken." (Deut. 24:5.)

When a loan was made, it was customary in Israel to require an article as a pledge—a guarantee or security. Note how carefully the law guarded the rights of the person seeking the loan, traditionally the vulnerable party in such an arrangement:

No man shall take the nether or the upper millstone to pledge: for he taketh a man's life to pledge. . . .

When thou dost lend thy brother any thing, thou shalt not go into his house to fetch his pledge. [In other words, the lender cannot appraise all of the items in the house under pretext of securing just the pledge offered by the borrower.]

Thou shalt stand abroad, and the man to whom thou dost lend shall bring out the pledge abroad unto thee.

And if the man be poor, thou shalt not sleep with his pledge:

In any case thou shalt deliver him the pledge again when the sun goeth down, that he may sleep in his own raiment, and bless thee: and it shall be righteousness unto thee before the Lord thy God. (Deut. 24:6, 10-13.)

Thus, if the pledge were an article of clothing, as it very well might be, the law would foresee the possibility that it might be his only spare article, or the blanket from the bed, and guarantee the family's comfort during the night.

Mosaic law was scrupulous in considering the poor and their needs:

> Thou shalt not oppress an hired servant that is poor and needy, whether he be of thy brethren, or of thy strangers that are in thy land within thy gates:
>
> At [the end of] his day thou shalt give him his hire, neither shall the sun go down upon it; for he is poor, and setteth his heart upon it: lest he cry against thee unto the Lord, and it be sin unto thee. (Deut. 24:14-15.)
>
> Thou shalt not have in thy bag divers weights, a great and a small.
>
> Thou shalt not have in thine house divers measures, a great and a small.
>
> But thou shalt have a perfect and just weight, a perfect and just measure shalt thou have: that thy days may be lengthened in the land which the Lord thy God giveth thee. (Deut. 25:13-15.)
>
> Thou shalt not wrest judgment; thou shalt not respect persons, neither take a gift: for a gift doth blind the eyes of the wise, and pervert the words of the righteous. (Deut. 16:19.)
>
> Ye shall not steal, neither deal falsely, neither lie one to another. . . .
>
> Ye shall do no unrighteousness in judgment: thou shalt not respect the person of the poor, nor honour the person of the mighty: but in righteousness shalt thou judge thy neighbour. (Lev. 19:11, 15.)

Thus, according to the measure of this law, what it meant to be honest in the everyday life of Israel is abundantly clear. We need sermons today that are equally applicable to our time and circumstances.

The law is unusual in singling out the handicapped

and marginal and specifying their rights. As I have already quoted:

Thou shalt not curse the deaf, nor put a stumblingblock before the blind, but shalt fear thy God: I am the Lord. (Lev. 19:14.)

And when ye reap the harvest of your land, thou shalt not wholly reap the corners of thy field, neither shalt thou gather the gleanings of thy harvest.

And thou shalt not glean thy vineyard, neither shalt thou gather every grape of thy vineyard; thou shalt leave them for the poor and stranger: I am the Lord your God. (Lev. 19: 9-10.)

If there be among you a poor man of one of thy brethren within any of thy gates in thy land which the Lord thy God giveth thee, thou shalt not harden thine heart, nor shut thine hand from thy poor brother:

But thou shalt open thine hand wide unto him, and shalt surely lend him sufficient for his need, in that which he wanteth.

Beware that there be not a thought in thy wicked heart, saying, The seventh year, the year of release, is at hand; and thine eye be evil against thy poor brother, and thou givest him nought; and he cry unto the Lord against thee, and it be sin unto thee.

Thou shalt surely give him, and thine heart shall not be grieved when thou givest unto him: because that for this thing the Lord thy God shall bless thee in all thy works, and in all that thou puttest thine hand unto.

For the poor shall never cease out of the land: therefore I command thee, saying, Thou shalt open thine hand wide unto thy brother, to thy poor, and to thy needy, in thy land.

And if thy brother, an Hebrew man, or an Hebrew woman, be sold unto thee, and serve thee six years; then in the seventh year thou shalt let him go free from thee.

And when thou sendest him out free from thee, thou shalt not let him go away empty:

Thou shalt furnish him liberally out of thy flock, and out of thy floor, and out of thy winepress: of that wherewith the Lord thy God hath blessed thee thou shalt give unto him.

85

> And thou shalt remember that thou wast a bondman in the land of Egypt, and the Lord thy God redeemed thee: therefore I command thee this thing to day. (Deut. 15:7-15.)

Many sections of the Mosaic law seem very harsh to us today. Our own moral sensitivity, for instance, would reject the law that allows parents to impose the death penalty on a rebellious child:

> If a man have a stubborn and rebellious son, which will not obey the voice of his father, or the voice of his mother, and that, when they have chastened him, will not hearken unto them:
> Then shall his father and his mother lay hold on him, and bring him out unto the elders of his city, and unto the gate of his place;
> And they shall say unto the elders of his city, This our son is stubborn and rebellious, he will not obey our voice; he is a glutton, and a drunkard.
> And all the men of his city shall stone him with stones, that he die: so shalt thou put evil away from among you; and all Israel shall hear, and fear. (Deut. 21:18-21.)

It also seems unfeeling and uncompassionate to obey the law that forbids an illegitimate child to "enter into the congregation of the Lord; even to his tenth generation." (Deut. 23:2.)

Our democratic traditions of equity would be opposed to the differential treatment allowed between "strangers" and Israelites in some circumstances: "Unto a stranger thou mayest lend upon usury; but unto thy brother thou shalt not lend upon usury: that the Lord thy God may bless thee in all that thou settest thine hand to in the land whither thou goest to possess it." (Deut. 23:20.)

The law that a childless widow must be married to her husband's brother so that the firstborn son may continue the dead man's name in Israel is another custom that we would find repugnant, especially since there is a way provided whereby a reluctant brother may escape

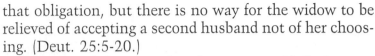

that obligation, but there is no way for the widow to be relieved of accepting a second husband not of her choosing. (Deut. 25:5-20.)

Despite such examples that we would find unacceptable, we must also remember that this was a society that did not have an elaborate system of prisons, correctional institutions, and courts. If someone committed a wrong, the trial and the punishment needed to be swift and decisive, for rehabilitation through incarceration is a modern development.

The penalties prescribed in the law were harsh enough to serve as deterrents and, even when they caused permanent maiming, served the purpose of both being a dreadful sort of visual aid against crime for others and deliberately hampering the criminal in repeating the same crime. But even at their extreme, there were often safeguards and protections against wanton cruelty or sadism. For instance, a frequent punishment for a criminal was a physical beating, but it was administered promptly in the presence of the judge who had ordered it, and the number of blows was prescribed by law:

> If there be a controversy between men, and they come unto judgment, that the judges may judge them; then they shall justify the righteous, and condemn the wicked.
>
> And it shall be, if the wicked man be worthy to be beaten, that the judge shall cause him to lie down, and to be beaten before his face, according to his fault, by a certain number.
>
> Forty stripes he may give him, and not exceed: lest, if he should exceed, and beat him above these with many stripes, then thy brother should seem vile unto thee. (Deut. 25:1-3.)

Although I applaud the humanness and the optimistic view of human nature that underlies our own judicial and correctional system, with its intense and appropriate concern for safeguarding the rights of the accused, it seems to me that it suffers greatly from the delays that clog our court calendars, from the invisible nature of much of the correction which means that our society as a whole has little interest in the criminal or in his or her rehabilitation, and in the impersonal nature of much of the punishment. Deuteronomy describes a system that does not suffer from vagueness or dilatory trials and punishment.

I am also interested in another rule that governed even the treatment of women captured during war. Aside from the modern Geneva Convention, which makes some minimal efforts toward protecting the rights of civilians, and the medieval code of chivalry, which operated in the case of well-born Christian women (but not lower-class or non-Christian women), I am not familiar with other systems that spelled out the rights of captive women, rather than simply treating them as the legitimate booty of the conquerors. This law does not attempt to safeguard such a woman's chastity, but it requires her captor to marry her and forbids him to sell her if he is not pleased. No doubt such requirements produced some happy unions, despite their violent beginnings:

> When thou goest forth to war against thine enemies, and the Lord thy God hath delivered them into thine hands, and thou hast taken them captive,
>
> And seest among the captives a beautiful woman, and hast a desire unto her, that thou wouldst have her to thy wife;
>
> Then thou shalt bring her home to thine house; and she shall shave her head, and pare her nails;
>
> And she shall put the raiment of her captivity from off her, and shall remain in thine house, and bewail her father and her mother a full month: and after that thou shalt go in unto her, and be her husband, and she shall be thy wife.
>
> And it shall be, if thou have no delight in her, then thou shalt let her go whither she will; but thou shalt not sell her at all for money, thou shalt not make merchandise of her, because thou hast humbled her. (Deut. 21:10-14.)

The Mosaic law is a highly personal expression. The

repetition of the formula "For I am the ~~Lor~~ should be a constant reminder that the law was a between God and his people, to keep their relationsh with him and with each other perfect and righteous. That accounts, in my opinion, for the absolute prohibitions against "divination, or [being] an observer of times, or an enchanter, or a witch, or a charmer, or a consulter with familiar spirits, or a wizard, or a necromancer. . . . Thou shalt be perfect with the Lord thy God." (Deut. 18:10-11, 13.) The law also, when used properly, will protect the people against false prophets:

> If there arise among you a prophet, or a dreamer of dreams, and giveth thee a sign or a wonder,
> And the sign or the wonder come to pass, whereof he spake unto thee, saying, Let us go after other gods, which thou hast not known, and let us serve them;
> Thou shalt not hearken unto the words of that prophet, or that dreamer of dreams: for the Lord your God proveth you, to know whether ye love the Lord your God with all your heart and with all your soul.
> Ye shall walk after the Lord your God, and fear him, and keep his commandments, and obey his voice, and ye shall serve him, and cleave unto him.
> And that prophet, or that dreamer of dreams, shall be put to death; because he hath spoken to turn you away from the Lord your God, which brought you out of the land of Egypt, and redeemed you out of the house of bondage, to thrust thee out of the way which the Lord thy God commanded thee to walk in. So shalt thou put the evil away from the midst of thee. (Deut. 13:1-5.)

Thus, considering the time and the circumstances, the Mosaic law outlined in the Old Testament is a remarkable document. It is just, merciful, quite humane, rational, and above all concrete and specific in its application to the issues of daily life.

The strength of the Christian ethic taught by Jesus lies in its positive emphasis on principle, leaving to us the method of applying the principle in our daily walk. Often, the high-sounding principle satisfies us and, because we do not actively do evil, we fail to practice our Christian love in concrete ways. The finer ethical-religious life, I believe, would be to combine the strengths of both the Judaic and the Christian ethics, being guided by principle and taking specific, positive ethical action in the marketplace, in the community, in the family, and among nations.

Chapter 15

THE WISDOM OF PROVERBS

The Old Testament book of Proverbs is traditionally ascribed to Solomon, a king extolled for his wisdom. It was an ancient custom to assign authorship to a famous character, no matter who wrote it. However, most scholars believe that Proverbs, like Psalms, is a collection of sayings amassed through the centuries. Clearly, it represents the practical wisdom of many Israelite thinkers, as well as the common sense of the people. Certainly, Solomon was foolish as well as wise, for he multiplied wives, horses, and taxes — an inevitably oppressive system that led to the division of the kingdom of Israel at his death.

Interesting and rich in subject matter, Proverbs contains much of value in its observations of daily living. Many of its passages are meaningful to me, but I would encourage readers to peruse Proverbs often and thoughtfully, with their needs in mind. This chapter contains some of my favorites.

As one who believes firmly in the collective wisdom and good of human beings, I appreciate Proverbs 11:14: "Where no counsel is, the people fall: but in the multitude of counsellors there is safety." Similar in expression and

91

intent is Proverbs 19:18: "Where there is no vision, the people perish."

I have often seen the damage done to human relationships by people who talk without thinking, gossip, or pass on perfectly true but quite unnecessary information. These two proverbs speak to that matter: "He that covereth a transgression seeketh love; but he that repeateth a matter separateth very friends" (17:9), and "As a jewel of gold in a swine's snout, so is a fair woman which is without discretion" (11:22). This latter proverb applies equally to men, of course.

I must admit that I cannot read the following very sound advice without feeling that the writer must have had a twinkle in his eye:

> He that hath knowledge spareth his words: and a man of understanding is of an excellent spirit.
> Even a fool, when he holdeth his peace, is counted wise: and he that shutteth his lips is esteemed a man of understanding." (17:27-28.)

In the same vein is this trenchant advice against rationalization:

> The way of a fool is right in his own eyes: but he that hearkeneth unto counsel is wise. (12:15.)
> There is a way which seemeth right unto a man, but the end thereof are the ways of death. (14:12.)
> All the ways of a man are clean in his own eyes; but the Lord weigheth the spirits. . . .
> A man's heart deviseth his way: but the Lord directeth his steps. (16:2, 9.)

It is hard to continue self-deceit with the reminder of Proverbs that the Lord not only sees what we are doing but also sees into our hearts and knows why.

A related form of self-control is that over one's temper. "A soft answer turneth away wrath," reminds the ever-practical Proverbs, "but grievous words stir up anger.

. . . He that is slow to anger is better than the mighty; and he that ruleth his spirit than he that taketh a city." (15:1; 16:32.)

I also like the way in which Proverbs urges humility and a correct evaluation of our own relationship with God: "Pride goeth before destruction, and an haughty spirit before a fall" (16:18); and "The fear of the Lord is the beginning of wisdom: and the knowledge of the holy is understanding" (9:10).

One of the longer sustained passages in Proverbs is an exposition of wisdom, which has been defined as the application of knowledge to good ends. It is to be found, according to Proverbs, in fear of the Lord, in knowledge of the holy, and in obedience to the Lord's will:

> Happy is the man that findeth wisdom, and the man that getteth understanding.
>
> For the merchandise of it is better than the merchandise of silver, and the gain thereof than fine gold.
>
> She is more precious than rubies: and all the things thou canst desire are not to be compared unto her.
>
> Length of days is in her right hand; and in her left hand riches and honour.
>
> Her ways are ways of pleasantness, and all her paths are peace.
>
> She is a tree of life to them that lay hold upon her: and happy is every one that retaineth her. (3:13-18.)
>
> Get wisdom, get understanding: forget it not; neither decline from the words of my mouth.
>
> Forsake her not, and she shall preserve thee: love her, and she shall keep thee.
>
> Wisdom is the principal thing; therefore get wisdom: and with all thy getting get understanding.
>
> Exalt her, and she shall promote thee: she shall bring thee to honour, when thou dost embrace her.
>
> She shall give to thine head an ornament of grace: a crown of glory shall she deliver to thee. (4:5-9.)

It is no small matter, in a world that honors and

rewards materialism with yet more material goods, to hear the echo of such words often in our minds.

Closely related — and equally a theme in Proverbs — is the issue of integrity. We are accustomed to thinking of this problem in the New Testament terms of being "in the world" without being "of the world." Proverbs talks of more than independence of judgment and intellect, however. It describes a kind of wholeheartedness that, again in New Testament terms, makes it possible to make our offerings to the Savior in an acceptable sacrifice. I think that the reason such a sacrifice is phrased in terms of a "broken heart" is that we, without thinking or without realizing the implication of our actions, "give" parts of our heart to unworthy ends and goals; then, when the desire comes to turn to the Savior and seek his atonement, we realize too late that we have "set" our hearts "so much on the things of the world" (D&C 121:35) that we can only shatter their hold on us by breaking our hearts before the Lord.

Much of the wisdom of making careful choices about where to give our hearts comes to me in this discussion from Proverbs:

> Keep thy heart with all diligence; for out of it are the issues of life.
>
> Put away from thee a froward mouth, and perverse lips put far from thee.
>
> Let thine eyes look right on, and let thine eyelids look straight before thee.
>
> Ponder the path of thy feet, and let all thy ways be established.
>
> Turn not to the right hand nor to the left: remove thy foot from evil. (4:23-27.)

Integrity embraces many virtues of life: honesty, humility, sincerity, meekness, and moral courage. It brings inner strength, peace of mind, and self-forgetfulness in service. I believe that we cannot offer anyone real love —

not another individual and not the Savior—without integrity.

Less lofty, perhaps, but not less essential in easing the sometimes difficult process of living and working together is good nature. Proverbs 18:14 points out: "The spirit of a man will sustain his [physical] infirmity; but a wounded spirit who can bear?" The question is obviously rhetorical. An earlier chapter in Proverbs responds to the same theme:

> A merry heart maketh a cheerful countenance: but by sorrow of the heart the spirit is broken. . . .
> All the days of the afflicted are evil: but he that is of a merry heart hath a continual feast. . . .
> Better is a dinner of herbs where love is, than a stalled ox and hatred therewith. (15:13, 15, 17.)

Why be defeated twice—once by circumstances and again by our attitude toward the event? Proverbs teaches us to face life with courage and good cheer.

Another important lesson taught by Proverbs is the value of work. A woman of my acquaintance who, laid up with a broken leg, watched television soap operas for a couple of weeks observed wryly at the end, "Quarreling, scrapping, falling in love, falling out, lawsuits, murder, depression, suicide—if those people had to actually work eight hours a day, they wouldn't have been in nearly so much trouble." I heartily concur. One of the great values of work is that it prevents people with small or perverse imaginations from getting in a great deal of trouble.

I deal often with the unfortunate, including the aged, the handicapped, and those who for one reason or another—many of them legitimate, some of them not—are not fully prepared to deal with the world. I see many legitimate cases of "hard luck," but I must say that I have seen many other cases where, rather than pleading hard luck, an individual has instead substituted hard work, with the result that he or she is not among those

95

who desire or need the assistance of others in making a way through the world. Proverbs 6:6-11 reminds us all:

> Go to the ant, thou sluggard; consider her ways, and be wise: which having no guide, overseer, or ruler,
>
> Provideth her meat in the summer, and gathereth her food in the harvest.
>
> How long wilt thou sleep, O sluggard? when wilt thou arise out of thy sleep?
>
> Yet a little sleep, a little slumber, a little folding of the hands to sleep:
>
> So shall thy poverty come as one that travelleth, and thy want as an armed man.

One of the most powerful warnings against self-indulgence as it applies to drinking occurs in Proverbs 23. I like to pair this passage with the Word of Wisdom and its promises in Doctrine and Covenants 89 because Proverbs unsparingly shows the punishment that accompanies drunkenness:

> Be not among winebibbers; among riotous eaters. . . .
>
> Who hath woe? who hath sorrow? who hath contentions? who hath babbling? who hath wounds without cause? who hath redness of eyes?
>
> They that tarry long at the wine; they that go to seek mixed wine.
>
> Look not thou upon the wine when it is red, when it giveth his colour in the cup, when it moveth itself aright.
>
> At the last it biteth like a serpent, and stingeth like an adder.
>
> Thine eyes shall behold strange women, and thine heart shall utter perverse things.
>
> Yea, thou shalt be as he that lieth down in the midst of the sea, or as he that lieth upon the top of a mast.
>
> They have stricken me, shalt thou say, and I was not sick; they have beaten me, and I felt it not: when shall I awake? I will seek it yet again. (23:29-35.)

Proverbs also makes a strong case for moderation,

not only for the beauty of the principle but also because excess leads to sin:

> Remove far from me vanity and lies: give me neither poverty nor riches; feed me with food convenient for me:
> Lest I be full, and deny thee, and say, who is the Lord? or lest I be poor, and steal, and take the name of my God in vain. (30:8-9.)

At least once a year, we can count on hearing a chapter of Proverbs read with fervor over the pulpit. It is Proverbs 31:10-31, which begins, "Who can find a virtuous woman? for her price is far above rubies." There are so few passages praising women in the scriptures that Mother's Day speakers often seize on this particular passage avidly. I, too, enjoy this passage, praising a woman who is so reliable that "the heart of her husband doth safely trust in her," who "do[es] him good and not evil," who weaves wool and flax, rises to her day's work before dawn and ends it long after dark, invests her money wisely, is provident and thrifty, wise and pious. Her husband "is known in the gates, when he sitteth among the elders of the land."

It seems likely to me that this passage could have been written by a man who wanted to be well provided for by a hard-working wife but who perhaps was less willing to expend the same effort himself. It also seems to me that this ancient ideal lacks any sense that women also need intellectual, social, and spiritual fulfillment. I am not sure, looking at the average congregation of Latter-day Saint mothers, that they need to be told to stay up later, get up earlier, or work harder than they are already doing.

However, the book of Proverbs, even as this example shows, is a revelation of human nature. It is not to be absorbed in one sitting but can feed us again and again as we return to it with different needs.

Chapter 16

THE REALISM OF ECCLESIASTES

Ecclesiastes, like Proverbs or the Psalms, is a collection of aphorisms or miscellaneous sayings on a variety of topics interspersed with a few longer passages on several subjects. However, it differs in many ways from the other books of the Old Testament. It is pessimistic in tone, in contrast to the sturdy optimism of Proverbs. The hope, faith, and purpose found in other books of the Old Testament are also absent. A repeated refrain is "all is vanity," sometimes translated as "all is emptiness" (as in the New English Bible) or "all is futility."

The God of Ecclesiastes is remote and unfathomable—a decided change from the God of the prophets who is deeply and compassionately concerned with human beings. The book is not unified nor are its ideas wholly consistent with each other. Nevertheless, I am glad that this book was incorporated into the Old Testament canon because of the aesthetic quality of its writing and also because its very pessimism throws into high relief the sense of joy and trust running under the other books. Consider, for example, this well-known passage:

> To every thing there is a season, and a time to every purpose under the heaven:

A time to be born, and a time to die; a time to plant, and a time to pluck up that which is planted;

A time to kill, and a time to heal; a time to break down, and a time to build up;

A time to weep, and a time to laugh; a time to mourn, and a time to dance;

A time to cast away stones, and a time to gather stones together; a time to embrace, and a time to refrain from embracing;

A time to get, and a time to lose; a time to keep, and a time to cast away;

A time to rend, and a time to sew; a time to keep silence, and a time to speak;

A time to love, and a time to hate; a time of war, and a time of peace. (Eccl. 3:1-8.)

While it may first strike us as shocking to think of a time to kill or a time to hate, the basic idea expressed in these verses is sound. Change is the stuff of life. Attempting to make rules or philosophical systems that will prevent change from occurring—insisting either internally or aloud that something must always be the same—is a futile endeavor, one that denies the "season" of each life stage.

Youth and early adulthood are the time to get an education and vocational training as an economic foundation for the rest of one's life. The twenties are a good time in our culture to marry and begin a family. Even old age, which cannot be changed or overcome, should be accepted with grace.

It is appropriate to work at times and to play at others, to laugh at some events and to weep at others. It is part of life to win and to lose, to have good fortune and bad luck. The message of this passage is to take these changes with gratitude and with courage, accepting whatever comes until it can be changed or overcome—or until it simply gives way to a new part of the cycle.

At first glance, the author of Ecclesiastes would seem

to contradict himself and this celebration of change by writing a bitterly pessimistic passage like this:

> Then said I in my heart, As it happeneth to the fool, so it happeneth even to me; and why was I then more wise? Then I said in my heart, that this also is vanity.
>
> For there is no remembrance of the wise more than of the fool for ever; seeing that which now is in the days to come shall all be forgotten. And how dieth the wise man? as the fool.
>
> Therefore I hated life; because the work that is wrought under the sun is grievous unto me: for all is vanity and vexation of spirit.
>
> Yea, I hated all my labour which I had taken under the sun: because I should leave it unto the man that shall be after me. (2:15-18.)

I feel that, rather than contradiction, we see here an important part of the cycle. Many times the relinquishment and resignation that precede acceptance come only when there is a period of disillusionment or disappointment that makes us stop and think. Our natural inclination is to behave as we have always behaved, to think that things not only will but *should* remain the same. Sometimes the fact that things have already changed must forcibly confront our desires. In the shock that follows, disappointment and discouragement are natural feelings. But out of them may come a new acceptance and a new integration of our life's values that accommodate and simultaneously rise above our previous understanding.

As I continue to add full, rich years to those that have already gone before, I perceive also the limitations that those years bring and accept the inevitability of the end of my own life. I think that Ecclesiastes must be a sympathetic voice to many people who are beginning to understand that death may be delayed but not defeated, and that it is the common end of us all. After all our particular experiences, death is the great universal experience through which we each must pass but which none of us can fully share with another:

> For that which befalleth the sons of men befalleth beasts; even one thing befalleth them: as the one dieth, so dieth the other; yea, they have all one breath; so that a man hath no preeminence above a beast: for all is vanity.
>
> All go unto one place; all are of the dust, and all turn to dust again.
>
> Who knoweth the spirit of man that goeth upward, and the spirit of the beast that goeth downward to the earth? (3:19-21.)
>
> For all this I considered in my own heart even to declare all this, that the righteous, and the wise, and their works, are in the hand of God: no man knoweth either love or hatred by all that is before them.
>
> All things come alike to all: there is one event to the righteous, and to the wicked; to the good and to the clean, and to the unclean; to him that sacrificeth, and to him that sacrificeth not: as is the good, so is the sinner; and he that sweareth, as he that feareth an oath.
>
> This is an evil among all things that are done under the sun, that there is one event unto all: yea, also the heart of the sons of men is full of evil, and madness is in their heart while they live, and after that they go to the dead.
>
> For to him that is joined to all the living there is hope: for a living dog is better than a dead lion.
>
> For the living know that they shall die: but the dead know not any thing, neither have they any more a reward; for the memory of them is forgotten.
>
> Also their love, and their hatred, and their envy, is now perished; neither have they any more a portion for ever in any thing that is done under the sun. . . .
>
> I returned, and saw under the sun, that the race is not to the swift, nor the battle to the strong, neither yet bread to the wise, nor yet riches to men of understanding, nor yet favour to men of skill; but time and chance happeneth to them all.
>
> For man also knoweth not his time: as the fishes that

are taken in an evil net, and as the birds that are caught in the snare; so are the sons of men snared in an evil time, when it falleth suddenly upon them. (9:1-6, 11-12.)

There is much truth in the author's description, bitter though it may seem, that death removes us from our best efforts and the arenas of action where we have been used to taking charge. All people are subject to the same laws of nature. Volcanoes, earthquakes, and hurricanes strike at random. Heart disease attacks saint and sinner alike. The drunken driver can run anyone down. Death comes to all. Nature eventually gets the upper hand. The most powerful general and the wisest mother die like everyone else.

Although it is true that none of us can claim exemption from trouble, risk, pain, and death, it is certainly true that the righteous person, the disciple of Christ, can be spared the suffering that comes from greed, selfishness, loneliness, hate, and dissipation.

Those who find the approach of Ecclesiastes' author oppressively negative would do well to remember that Jesus, in a more positive way, was equally realistic in recognizing the common experiences of humankind:

> But I say unto you, Love your enemies, bless them that curse you, do good to them that hate you, and pray for them which despitefully use you, and persecute you;
>
> That ye may be the children of your Father which is in heaven: for he maketh his sun to rise on the evil and on the good, and sendeth rain on the just and on the unjust. (Matt. 5:44-45.)
>
> Therefore whosoever heareth these sayings of mine, and doeth them, I will liken him unto a wise man, which built his house upon a rock:
>
> And the rain descended, and the floods came, and the winds blew, and beat upon that house; and it fell not: for it was founded upon a rock.
>
> And every one that heareth these sayings of mine, and

doeth them not, shall be likened unto a foolish man, which built his house upon the sand:

And the rain descended, and the floods came, and the winds blew, and beat upon that house; and it fell: and great was the fall of it. (Matt. 7:24-27.)

Religion is not an escape from the realities of life, but the power to deal with them with faith and equanimity. Ecclesiastes seems to miss the strength of that faith with such passages as this:

Wherefore I praised the dead which are already dead more than the living which are yet alive.

Yea, better is he than both they, which hath not yet been, who hath not seen the evil work that is done under the sun. (4:2-3.)

However, the author does not totally despair of life but instead admonishes us to make the most of it here and now:

Go thy way, eat thy bread with joy, and drink thy wine with a merry heart; for God now accepteth thy works.

Let thy garments be always white; and let thy head lack no ointment.

Live joyfully with the wife whom thou lovest all the days of . . . thy [life], which he hath given thee under the sun, . . . for that is thy portion in this life, and in thy labour which thou takest under the sun.

Whatsoever thy hand findeth to do, do it with thy might: for there is no work, nor device, nor knowledge, nor wisdom, in the grave whither thou goest. (9:7-10.)

The author freely recognizes the innocence of youth and its natural high spirits — also recognizing that both these good things can lead the unwary into temptation:

Rejoice, O young man, in thy youth; and let thy heart cheer thee in the days of thy youth, and walk in the ways of thine heart, and in the sight of thine eyes: but know thou, that for all these things God will bring thee into judgment.

Therefore remove sorrow from thy heart, and put away

evil from thy flesh: for childhood and youth are vanity. (11: 9-10.)

I find particular interest in the book's closing verses. First, the author observes: "Of making many books there is no end; and much study is a weariness of the flesh." (12:12.) Although this verse is addressed as "admonish[ment]" to "my son," it still strikes a note of humor with me, as though the author realizes that his book is one of those of which "there is no end." The final two verses, however, are profoundly religious — and one reason why I would encourage anyone who begins this book, with its pessimism and even cynicism, to continue reading to the end:

> Let us hear the conclusion of the whole matter: Fear God, and keep his commandments: for this is the whole duty of man.
> For God shall bring every work into judgment, with every secret thing, whether it be good, or whether it be evil. (12: 13-14.)

Chapter 17

THE PROBLEM OF SUFFERING: JOB

Many scholars consider the book of Job the greatest piece of religious literature ever written. It certainly has many of the hallmarks of good literature: a profound theme, concrete images, beautiful language, deep feeling, and a strongly portrayed leading character. It is clearly the work of a talented and subtle mind.

The book presents, in strong juxtaposition, two concepts in apparent opposition: the fact of unmerited human suffering and the goodness of God. Why do human beings suffer? Job's so-called friends argue that his sufferings are punishment for his sins and urge him to confess his sins, promising that his suffering will cease. Job strongly asserts his innocence and maintains the integrity of his moral life, demanding that God himself explain the paradox. At the end of the debate, God intervenes, rejects the false piety of Job's friends, and gives Job a new perspective.

The book opens with a prologue, chapters 1 and 2, which takes place in heaven. In it, God and Satan discuss Job's character, Satan arguing that Job is righteous only because he is happy, healthy, wealthy, and favored with a large family. He has every incentive to be righteous and none to be rebellious, but what, argues Satan, would he do if these gifts were taken away? Satan receives permission to destroy Job's children, flocks, and herds:

> Then Job arose, and rent his mantle, and shaved his head, and fell down upon the ground, and worshipped,
> And said, Naked came I out of my mother's womb, and naked shall I return thither: the Lord gave, and the Lord hath taken away; blessed be the name of the Lord.
> In all this Job sinned not, nor charged God foolishly. (1:20-22.)

Satan was then allowed to afflict Job with painful boils. At that point, even his wife bitterly incited him to "curse God and die."

> But he said unto her, Thou speakest as one of the foolish women speaketh. What? shall we receive good at the hand of God, and shall we not receive evil? In all this did not Job sin with his lips. (2:20.)

At this point, Job's three friends arrive and the philosophical debate begins. It seems reasonable to me to see the prologue as the unknown author's dramatic setting to heighten the human tensions around the issues that follow. However, it does not make good theology to interpret this prologue as literal fact. I do not believe that God permits Satan to kill members of our family, nor do I believe that Satan has the power to afflict us with physical ailments. This would violate our free agency and is unmerciful. Similarly, the epilogue (42:10-17), which has Job again receive ten children and even more flocks and herds, seems to make most sense as the addition of a pious scribe who wanted to restore Job to his original material prosperity. Again, it seems bad theology to equate prosperity with righteousness.

This issue aside, however, I believe that any reader

who comes to the debate through the setting of the prologue has a keener interest in the arguments of God's
goodness and the paradox of human suffering that make
up the body of the book. And there is a certain amount
of human satisfaction in the "happily ever after" quality
of the epilogue.

Although Job will not curse God, he expresses, in
some of the most beautiful and eloquent language in the
Old Testament, the misery of his existence through the
metaphor of regretting the day of his birth:

> Let the day perish wherein I was born, and the night in
> which it was said, There is a man child conceived.
> Let that day be darkness; let not God regard it from above,
> neither let the light shine upon it. (3:1-2.)

He continues in this vein for most of the chapter.
Then Eliphaz, Bildad, and Zophar approach, mourn with
Job, and probe for the causes of his misfortune, at first
cautiously and sympathetically, then more aggressively
until they are accusing Job and defending themselves.
Another sign that this book is deliberately constructed
by a gifted writer is the structure of the debate. Each
friend speaks and Job answers; this pattern is repeated
three times, forming a "three-round" debate.

In the first "round," chapters 4 through 14, Eliphaz
enunciates a traditional philosophy that the righteous
are somehow protected from misfortune and that only
the wicked suffer:

> Remember, I pray thee, who ever perished, being inno-
> cent? or where were the righteous cut off?
> Even as I have seen, they that plow iniquity, and sow
> wickedness, reap the same.
> By the blast of God they perish, and by the breath of his
> nostrils are they consumed. . . .
> Shall mortal man be more just than God? shall a man
> be more pure than his maker?

> Behold, he put no trust in his servants; and his angels he charged with folly:
> How much less in them that dwell in houses of clay, whose foundation is in the dust, which are crushed before the moth? (4:7-9, 17-19.)

Job protests this facile philosophy, which will convict him of guilt, adding to his emotional burdens:

> What doth your arguing reprove?
> Do ye imagine to reprove words, and the speeches of one that is desperate, which are as wind?
> Yea, ye overwhelm the fatherless, and ye dig a pit for your friend.
> . . . Look upon me; for it is evident unto you if I lie. (6: 24-28.)

He continues his defense through chapter 7, demanding to know what sins he has committed and insisting on his innocence.

Bildad, the second comforter, reiterates Eliphaz's perspective in chapter 8, repeating that Job must be suffering for his sins. In his reply in chapters 9 and 10, Job expresses his weariness, his confusion, and his lack of understanding of the ways of God. Raising his complaint to God, he again invokes his righteousness:

> My soul is weary of my life; I will leave my complaint upon myself; I will speak in the bitterness of my soul.
> I will say unto God, Do not condemn me; shew me wherefore thou contendest with me.
> Is it good unto thee that thou shouldest oppress, that thou shouldest despise the work of thine hands, and shine upon the counsel of the wicked?
> Hast thou eyes of flesh? or seest thou as man seeth?
> Are thy days as the days of man? are thy years as man's days,
> That thou enquirest after mine iniquity, and searchest after my sin?
> Thou knowest that I am not wicked; and there is none that can deliver out of thine hand.

Thine hands have made me and fashioned me together round about; yet thou dost destroy me. (10:1-8.)

In chapter 11, Zophar, the third friend, intensifies the attack on Job, brutally accusing him of hidden sin:

> Should thy lies make men hold their peace? and when thou mockest, shall no man make thee ashamed?
>
> For thou hast said, My doctrine is pure, and I am clean in thine eyes.
>
> But oh that God would speak, and open his lips against thee;
>
> And that he would shew thee the secrets of wisdom, that they are double to that which is! Know therefore that God exacteth of thee less than thine iniquity deserveth. (11:3-6.)

Goaded by these accusations, Job responds with equal passion, again returning to his relationship with God and seeking to understand why these changes have come about:

> Hold your peace, let me alone, that I may speak, and let come on me what will. . . .
>
> Though he slay me, yet will I trust in him: but I will maintain mine own ways before him. . . .
>
> How many are mine iniquities and sins? make me to know my transgression and my sin.
>
> Wherefore hidest thou thy face, and holdest me for thine enemy? (13:13, 15, 23-24.)

Then in an exquisite passage on the fragility of life, Job laments:

> Man that is born of a woman is of few days, and full of trouble.
>
> He cometh forth like a flower, and is cut down: he fleeth also as a shadow, and continueth not. . . .
>
> For there is hope of a tree, if it be cut down, that it will sprout again, and that the tender branch thereof will not cease.
>
> Though the root thereof wax old in the earth, and the stock thereof die in the ground;

111

> Yet through the scent of water it will bud, and bring forth boughs like a plant.
> But man dieth, and wasteth away: yea, man giveth up the ghost, and where is he?
> As the waters fail from the sea, and the flood decayeth and drieth up:
> So man lieth down, and riseth not: till the heavens be no more, they shall not awake, nor be raised out of their sleep. (14:1-2, 7-12.)

The second interchange, which covers chapters 15 through 21, sees a heightening of emotions. Eliphaz begins the second round. Apparently realizing that Job cannot reasonably be convicted of personal iniquity, he falls back on a general denunciation of all human beings as unrighteous creatures, thus accusing Job by virtue of accusing the entire human race:

> What is man, that he should be clean? and he which is born of a woman, that he should be righteous?
> Behold, he putteth no trust in his saints; yea, the heavens are not clean in his sight.
> How much more abominable and filthy is man, which drinketh iniquity like water? (15:14-16.)

At this point, Job does not respond directly to his friend's accusations but returns with renewed vigor to his suit against God. Courageously, he accuses God of injustice:

> Know now that God hath overthrown me, and hath compassed me with his net.
> Behold, I cry out of wrong, but I am not heard: I cry aloud, but there is no judgment.
> He hath fenced up my way that I cannot pass, and he hath set darkness in my paths.
> He hath stripped me of my glory, and taken the crown from my head. . . .
> Have pity upon me, have pity upon me, O ye my friends; for the hand of God hath touched me. (19:6-9, 21.)

Energetically he refutes the specious logic of his comforters, pointing out that there is no simple equation between sin and misfortune or between prosperity and righteousness:

> Wherefore do the wicked live, become old, yea, are mighty in power?
>
> Their seed is established in their sight with them, and their offspring before their eyes.
>
> Their houses are safe from fear, neither is the rod of God upon them.
>
> Their bull gendereth, and faileth not; their cow calveth, and casteth not her calf.
>
> They send forth their little ones like a flock, and their children dance.
>
> They take the timbrel and harp, and rejoice at the sound of the organ.
>
> They spend their days in wealth, and in a moment go down to the grave. (21:7-13.)

The same themes, with ingenious variations and unfailing eloquence, continue. In the third bout, chapters 22 through 31, Job sets aside his own bewilderment and anger—without abating one jot of his complaint against God—to powerfully affirm his faith as the moral center of his life:

> As God liveth, who hath taken away my judgment; and the Almighty, who hath vexed my soul;
>
> All the while my breath is in me, and the spirit of God is in my nostrils;
>
> My lips shall not speak wickedness, nor my tongue utter deceit.
>
> God forbid that I should justify you: till I die I will not remove mine integrity from me.
>
> My righteousness I hold fast, and will not let it go: my heart shall not reproach me so long as I live. (27:1-6.)

Elihu, the youngest and confessedly the least experienced of the friends, has a long speech (chapters 32–37), in which he affirms the wisdom and justice of God, counsels humility, and admits that he has no solution to the paradox of Job's situation.

At that point, in chapters 38 through 41, God intervenes, deluging Job with a dazzling catalogue of creative mysteries and unanswerable questions:

> Where wast thou when I laid the foundations of the earth? declare, if thou has understanding. . . .
> When the morning stars sang together, and all the sons of God shouted for joy? . . .
> Where is the way where light dwelleth? . . .
> Hath the rain a father? or who hath begotten the drops of dew?
> Out of whose womb came the ice? . . .
> Who hath put wisdom in the inward parts? or who hath given understanding to the heart?
> Knowest thou the time when the wild goats of the rock bring forth?
> Hast thou given the horse strength? hast thou clothed his neck with thunder? (38:4, 7, 19, 28-29, 36; 39:1, 19.)

Job, completely overwhelmed, no longer urges his claim on God's justice, but God does not convict him of impiety or lack of faith. Instead, it is the false reasoning of his friends that God categorically rejects: "The Lord said to Eliphaz the Temanite, My wrath is kindled against thee, and against thy two friends: for ye have not spoken of me the thing that is right, as my servant Job hath." (42:7.)

The effect is to let Job know—as Job is fully willing to admit, at this point—that he has a very limited perspective on life compared with God's. The question of why human beings suffer is not answered, except to make it clear that suffering cannot simply be equated with sinfulness. Rather, the teaching of the book of Job is to trust God, who knows and understands life from a different perspective than we do.

Chapter 18

THE BEAUTY
OF PURE WORSHIP:
THE PSALMS

Writers of the Old Testament often promise well-being and prosperity to those who obey divine commandments, and retribution and punishment to those who disobey or ignore God's laws. Deuteronomy 28 describes in eloquent detail the blessings that will follow the Israelites if they will "hearken diligently unto the voice of the Lord . . . to observe and to do all his commandments"—blessings of prosperity, protection, health, children, holiness, and power. But if they are disobedient, parallel curses will follow them: ill health, poverty, misery, plague, drought, "madness, and blindness, and astonishment of heart" (Deut. 28:28), the sorrows of the captive, frustration, the loss of children, work without fruit, servitude, and constant worry and unease:

> Moreover all these curses shall come upon thee, and shall pursue thee, and overtake thee, till thou be destroyed; because thou hearkenedst not unto the voice of the Lord thy God, to keep his commandments and his statutes which he commanded thee:

> And they shall be upon thee for a sign and for a wonder, and upon thy seed for ever.
>
> Because thou servedst not the Lord thy God with joyfulness, and with gladness of heart, for the abundance of all things. (Deut. 28:45-47.)

We hear a good deal in our day about keeping the commandments to receive blessings and avoid punishment. The Doctrine and Covenant teaches:

> There is a law, irrevocably decreed in heaven before the foundations of this world, upon which all blessings are predicated—
>
> And when we obtain any blessing from God, it is by obedience to that law upon which it is predicated. (D&C 130:20-21.)

There is an absolute logic about this statement. The commandments of God are the laws of life. The Word of Wisdom, generosity in sharing our material goods, diligence, fidelity, honesty, Christian love, and repentance bear good fruit. Obeying them brings their own reward. And the rewards of obedience are very specific. We obtain some measure of good health by obeying the known laws of health. By practicing safe, defensive driving, we arrive at our destinations safely. By keeping our integrity, we enjoy peace of mind. By loving our neighbors, we enjoy harmonious relations with others. To increase love, we give more and find new ways to serve.

But as we have learned from Job, reinforced by our own experience, righteous living guarantees no freedom from illness or misfortune. Cancer can strike anyone— sinner or saint. Furthermore, the desire for a blessing may not be the highest motive for obeying a law. A quid pro quo exchange of obedience for blessings is hardly the finest expression of religion. Self-concern will detract from the quality of our service for God and taint the purity of our worship. I do not think that God can be pleased with a believer who "keeps score" on his or her

116

own righteousness. Instead, I recommend to our attention the teachings of a little-known Old Testament prophet named Habakkuk. To me, he epitomizes pure worship.

Habakkuk witnessed the downfall of his people in the kingdom of Judah. While he acknowledged their sins, he was troubled because Babylon, a nation even more wicked, was permitted to take the Jews into captivity and to destroy the holy city of Jerusalem and its sacred temple. But his faith in the Lord was based not on his own welfare, but on his conception of God. Under any and all circumstances, he resolved, he would praise the Lord for his being:

> Although the fig tree shall not blossom, neither shall fruit be in the vines; the labour of the olive shall fail, and the fields shall yield no meat; the flock shall be cut off from the fold, and there shall be no herd in the stalls:
>
> Yet I will rejoice in the Lord, I will joy in the God of my salvation.
>
> The Lord God is my strength, and he will make my feet like hinds' feet, and he will make me to walk upon mine high places. (Hab. 3:17-19.)

Psalm 73 has much the same feeling. Its author recognizes that the wicked prosper, live untroubled, and "have more than heart could wish" (v. 7). How could such a thing be? The answer comes in the transcendant knowledge that shows a broader view than the limits of this life only and reassures him that God alone, who is beyond understanding, merits his worship and devotion:

> When I thought to know this, it was too painful for me;
>
> Until I went into the sanctuary of God; then understood I their end.
>
> Surely thou didst set them in slippery places; thou castedst them down into destruction. . . .
>
> So foolish was I, and ignorant: I was as a beast before thee.

> Nevertheless I am continually with thee: thou hast holden me by my right hand.
>
> Thou shalt guide me with thy counsel, and afterward receive me to glory.
>
> Whom have I in heaven but thee? and there is none upon earth that I desire beside thee.
>
> My flesh and my heart faileth: but God is the strength of my heart, and my portion for ever.
>
> For, lo, they that are far from thee shall perish: thou hast destroyed all them that go a whoring from thee.
>
> But it is good for me to draw near to God: I have put my trust in the Lord God, that I may declare all thy works. (Ps. 73:16-18, 22-28.)

Job learned in the end that, despite the tragedies of his life, he must keep faith with God and put his trust in him, trusting beyond understanding, trusting beyond reason, trusting despite the bewilderments and discrepancies of mortal existence.

Confucius, sage of ancient China, did not teach his people to worship God, but he certainly taught them to love and live the truth for its own sake — not out of fear, hope, or reward, or even as a duty. I find his statement delightful in its humility and humor:

> They who know the truth are not equal to those who love it, and they who love it are not equal to those who delight in it.
>
> At thirty I stood firm. At forty I had no doubts. At fifty I knew the decrees of heaven. At sixty my ear was an obedient organ for the reception of the truth. *At seventy I could follow what my heart desired without transgressing what was right.*

Our actions are certainly important, but so are the motives that move us to act. Our motivation varies from time to time and from deed to deed. I think it very likely that Confucius's behavior did not alter drastically between the time he was thirty and the time he was sixty, but that the deeper understandings he brought to those

behaviors and the purity of his motives made the differ
ence between mere obedience and true wisdom.

Or let's use the illustration of paying tithing. I doubt
very much that we always have the same reasons for
paying tithing throughout our lives. Sometimes we may
pay tithing out of fear of not being acceptable to the Lord.
Sometimes we may do it to receive the promised blessings
of prosperity. Sometimes we may feel it our duty, an
obligation to support the Church. Sometimes it is an act
of sheer faith, without even any hope that we will be
rewarded or that it will make a difference except to our
own integrity. And sometimes we pay tithing out of gratitude to God, freely, with no other motive.

The finest experiences of life are those which have
great meaning and value in and of themselves, irrespec-
tive of external values like what future good it could bring
or what others may think of us. I am thinking of such
things as friendship, the moments of looking deep into
the eyes of a beloved companion and realizing the blessings of a good marriage, enjoying a walk through a spring
garden, listening to the thunder and passion of Bee-
thoven, or drinking a glass of fresh orange juice on a hot
day. The more that life can be lived for its own sake, the
richer life is and the greater our own integrity. Our relationship to our Father in heaven and to Jesus belongs
in this category. They merit our whole-souled devotion.

Religion reaches its highest expression when we live
it — not for a reward either here or in heaven but because
it is true, it is good, and it is deserving of our loyalty and
love. Love of God, love of neighbor, and humility bring
their own rewards — but only if we do not seek them.
God is to be honored, revered, and loved for what he is —
for his own sake. Such is the message of Habakkuk and
the Psalmist.

Explore with me, if you will, the passion and exquisite
joy of the Psalms in their expression of wholehearted

praise and true worship. It seems most appropriate to me that they are attributed to David, an innocent but not helpless youth, who stood between danger and his father's sheep, who rejoiced in the beauties of the natural world around him, and whose pure voice and instinct for harmony could dispel even the evil spirit that troubled Saul. It is obvious from their content that many were written centuries after David's time but reflecting the same intimate worship of God and the same rejoicing in his creations.

It is also obvious that they were meant to be sung, accompanied by such musical instruments as the harp, viol, lyre, horn, trumpet, drums, or cymbals. I wish that we had the ancient settings for some of these lovely Psalms. I deeply appreciate the inspiration of modern composers who have created new and beautiful settings for some of them.

I have referred to the Psalms often in earlier chapters, for they are among my favorite scriptures in the Old Testament. If any of these, my favorites, appeal to you, let me suggest that you mark them in your own scriptures and continue to browse, making a treasure house of these rich expressions for yourself.

Psalm 8 expresses praise of human nature and gratitude to God for life:

> O Lord our Lord, how excellent is thy name in all the earth! who hast set thy glory above the heavens.
>
> Out of the mouth of babes and sucklings hast thou ordained strength because of thine enemies, that thou mightest still the enemy and the avenger.
>
> When I consider thy heavens, the work of thy fingers, the moon and the stars, which thou hast ordained;
>
> What is man, that thou art mindful of him? and the son of man, that thou visitest him?
>
> For thou hast made him a little lower than the angels, and hast crowned him with glory and honour.

> Thou madest him to have dominion over the works of thy hands; thou hast put all things under his feet:
> All sheep and oxen, yea, and the beasts of the field;
> The fowl of the air, and the fish of the sea, and whatsoever passeth through the paths of the seas.
> O Lord our Lord, how excellent is thy name in all the earth! (Ps. 8:1-9.)

I love the emphasis on ethics in the Psalms, which echoes that of the prophetic writings. Worship of God must be accompanied by righteous living:

> Lord, who shall abide in thy tabernacle? who shall dwell in thy holy hill?
> He that walketh uprightly, and worketh righteousness, and speaketh the truth in his heart.
> He that backbiteth not with his tongue, nor doeth evil to his neighbour, nor taketh up a reproach against his neighbour.
> In whose eyes a vile person is contemned; but he honoureth them that fear the Lord. He that sweareth to his own hurt, and changeth not.
> He that putteth not out his money to usury, nor taketh reward against the innocent. He that doeth these things shall never be moved. (Ps. 15.)

The sacred sense of the next verse communicates the Psalmist's sense of worship:

> The Lord is my light and my salvation; whom shall I fear? the Lord is the strength of my life; of whom shall I be afraid? (Ps. 27:1.)

I can believe that David composed Psalm 51. In his youth, he was an idealist. In later years, he committed adultery with the wife of a friend and brought about the friend's death. Nathan the prophet made David's sin vivid to him. That psalm is a cry of repentance:

> Have mercy upon me, O God, according to thy lovingkindness: according unto the multitude of thy tender mercies blot out my transgressions.

121

Wash me throughly from mine iniquity, and cleanse me from my sin.

For I acknowledge my transgressions: and my sin is ever before me.

Against thee, thee only, have I sinned, and done this evil in thy sight: that thou mightest be justified when thou speakest, and be clear when thou judgest.

Behold, I was shapen in iniquity; and in sin did my mother conceive me.

Behold, thou desirest truth in the inward parts: and in the hidden part thou shalt make me to know wisdom.

Purge me with hyssop, and I shall be clean: wash me, and I shall be whiter than snow.

Make me to hear joy and gladness; that the bones which thou hast broken may rejoice.

Hide thy face from my sins, and blot out all mine iniquities.

Create in me a clean heart, O God; and renew a right spirit within me.

Cast me not away from thy presence; and take not thy holy spirit from me.

Restore unto me the joy of thy salvation; and uphold me with thy free spirit.

Then will I teach transgressors thy ways; and sinners shall be converted unto thee.

Deliver me from bloodguiltiness, O God, thou God of my salvation: and my tongue shall sing aloud of thy righteousness.

O Lord, open thou my lips; and my mouth shall shew forth thy praise.

For thou desirest not sacrifice; else would I give it: thou delightest not in burnt offering.

The sacrifices of God are a broken spirit: a broken and a contrite heart, O God, thou wilt not despise. (Ps. 51:1-17.)

For God-centered worship, I like Psalms 96, 98, and 138:

Psalm 96

O sing unto the Lord a new song: sing unto the Lord, all the earth.

Sing unto the Lord, bless his name; shew forth his salvation from day to day.

Declare his glory among the heathen, his wonders among all people.

For the Lord is great, and greatly to be praised: he is to be feared above all gods.

For all the gods of the nations are idols: but the Lord made the heavens.

Honour and majesty are before him: strength and beauty are in his sanctuary.

Give unto the Lord, O ye kindreds of the people, give unto the Lord glory and strength.

Give unto the Lord the glory due unto his name: bring an offering, and come into his courts.

O worship the Lord in the beauty of holiness: fear before him, all the earth.

Say among the heathen that the Lord reigneth: the world also shall be established that it shall not be moved: he shall judge the people righteously.

Let the heavens rejoice, and let the earth be glad; let the sea roar, and the fulness thereof.

Let the field be joyful, and all that is therein: then shall all the trees of the wood rejoice

Before the Lord: for he cometh, for he cometh to judge the earth: he shall judge the world with righteousness, and the people with his truth.

Psalm 98

O sing unto the Lord a new song; for he hath done marvellous things: his right hand, and his holy arm, hath gotten him the victory.

The Lord hath made known his salvation: his righteousness hath he openly shewed in the sight of the heathen.

He hath remembered his mercy and his truth toward the house of Israel: all the ends of the earth have seen the salvation of our God.

Make a joyful noise unto the Lord, all the earth: make a loud noise, and rejoice, and sing praise.

Sing unto the Lord with the harp; with the harp, and the voice of a psalm.

With trumpets and sound of cornet make a joyful noise before the Lord, the King.

Let the sea roar, and the fulness thereof; the world, and they that dwell therein.

Let the floods clap their hands: let the hills be joyful together

Before the Lord; for he cometh to judge the earth: with righteousness shall he judge the world, and the people with equity.

Psalm 138

I will praise thee with my whole heart: before the gods will I sing praise unto thee.

I will worship toward thy holy temple, and praise thy name for thy lovingkindness and for thy truth: for thou hast magnified thy word above all thy name.

In the day when I cried thou answeredst me, and strengthenedst me with strength in my soul.

All the kings of the earth shall praise thee, O Lord, when they hear the words of thy mouth.

Yea, they shall sing in the ways of the Lord: for great is the glory of the Lord.

Though the Lord be high, yet hath he respect unto the lowly: but the proud he knoweth afar off.

Though I walk in the midst of trouble, thou wilt revive me: thou shalt stretch forth thine hand against the wrath of mine enemies, and thy right hand shall save me.

The Lord will perfect that which concerneth me: thy mercy, O Lord, endureth for ever: forsake not the works of thine own hands.

Two of the supreme expressions of trust in the Lord's loving care are in the Psalms:

Whither shall I go from thy spirit? or whither shall I flee from thy presence?

If I ascend up into heaven, thou art there: if I make my bed in hell, behold, thou art there.

If I take the wings of the morning, and dwell in the uttermost parts of the sea;

Even there shall thy hand lead me, and thy right hand shall hold me.

If I say, Surely the darkness shall cover me; even the night shall be light about me.

Yea, the darkness hideth not from thee; but the night shineth as the day: the darkness and the light are both alike to thee. (Ps. 139:7-12.)

The other is equally beautiful and even better known:

The Lord is my shepherd; I shall not want

He maketh me to lie down in green pastures: he leadeth me beside the still waters.

He restoreth my soul: he leadeth me in the paths of righteousness for his name's sake.

Yea, though I walk through the valley of the shadow of death, I will fear no evil: for thou art with me; thy rod and thy staff they comfort me.

Thou preparest a table before me in the presence of mine enemies: thou anointest my head with oil; my cup runneth over.

Surely goodness and mercy shall follow me all the days of my life: and I will dwell in the house of the Lord for ever. (Ps. 23.)

In modern life, the Psalms are seldom used for devotional purposes except privately, with the exception of those that have been set to modern arrangements. I cannot read "The Lord is my light and my salvation; whom shall I fear? the Lord is the strength of my life; of whom shall I be afraid?" (Ps. 27:1) without having the stirring strains of music also go through my mind.

Many of our hymns are similarly God-centered and amount to genuine expression of worship and rejoicing. We need to think about how we can praise the Lord in our time and culture, for the heart desires to give voice in suitable expressions as well as befitting actions.

What a joy it is to feast upon the Psalms! To live with such words is to live with "the beauty of holiness" and the power of pure worship. Surely every life would be richer for such companions.

Part IV

SOCIAL PHILOSOPHY
IN THE OLD TESTAMENT

Chapter 19

THE QUESTION OF POWER: A TRANSCENDENTAL REFERENT

One of the most persistent problems in human relationships is that of domination. Who has the power to
rule over others, and what is the basis of that power?

Historically, political power has been held most often
by individuals rather than collectively—by kings, dicta-
tors, judges, or priests. It has often claimed as the basis
of its authority the will of the gods or the duty to protect
the more helpless from the domination of others, but
such noble goals have all too often been at the mercy of
simple human greed and desire for power.

Israel abandoned its prophets for kings, but seldom
had an absolute monarchy for long periods of time. Instead, the authority of the king was always held in tension
with—and sometimes against—the authority of the
prophets who stood outside the system and retained the
power to call it to account. It referred itself to a transcendent control unique in human history. We see in
this system the beginning of the checks and balances
system built into every functioning democracy today.

Authority to control or govern others is a difficult power to exercise wisely and in the interest of the governed. Lord Acton's epigram still rings true: "Power corrupts, and absolute power corrupts absolutely." Equally true is its modern variant: "Power attracts corruptibility, and absolute power attracts absolute corruptibility." Hitler, Mussolini, and Stalin all demonstrated the spiral of evil that can be set in motion by power operating to accrue more power.

In that remarkable modern revelation on how the priesthood should be exercised, we read: "We have learned by sad experience that it is the nature and disposition of almost all men, as soon as they get a little authority, as they suppose, they will immediately begin to exercise unrighteous dominion." (D&C 121:39.)

If this insight is true in the idealistic setting of the gospel and the Church, how much truer is it of authority in the political and social arena!

Beginning with Saul, Israel gave its allegiance to kings, both in the united kingdom under Saul, David, and Solomon, and then in the divided kingdoms of Israel and Judah until their respective captivities by Assyria in 722 B.C. and Babylonia in 586 B.C. Unlike kings elsewhere in the world, the rulers of Israel were not laws unto themselves, though some tried to be. They were monitored by prophets of God who, as God's spokesmen, interpreted his will.

As early as the days of Moses, the Israelites had been warned of the difficulties monarchs would bring upon the people:

> When thou art come unto the land which the Lord thy God giveth thee, and shalt possess it, and shalt dwell therein, and shalt say, I will set a king over me, like as all the nations that are about me;
> Thou shalt in any wise set him king over thee, whom the Lord thy God shall choose: one from among thy brethren

shalt thou set king over thee: thou mayest not set a stranger over thee, which is not thy brother.

But he shall not multiply horses to himself, nor cause the people to return to Egypt, to the end that he should multiply horses: forasmuch as the Lord hath said unto you, Ye shall henceforth return no more that way.

Neither shall he multiply wives to himself, that his heart turn not away: neither shall he greatly multiply to himself silver and gold.

And it shall be, when he sitteth upon the throne of his kingdom, that he shall write him a copy of this law in a book out of that which is before the priests the Levites:

And it shall be with him, and he shall read therein all the days of his life: that he may learn to fear the Lord his God, to keep all the words of this law and these statutes, to do them:

That his heart be not lifted up above his brethren, and that he turn not aside from the commandment, to the right hand, or to the left: to the end that he may prolong his days in his kingdom, he, and his children, in the midst of Israel. (Deut. 17:14-20.)

Despite this antimonarchial tradition, the diverse tribes of Israel both wanted and needed a king—rather than judges who were periodically "raised up"—to unify them, to help them protect themselves against competing tribes and countries, and to give them more concrete identity as a nation. Samuel, a prophet of God, acting on God's instructions, chose Saul and anointed him king of Israel, but monitored his actions closely and terminated his reign because of disobedience. (1 Sam. 15.) His rebuke to the erring king, even though Samuel had violated his own obligation to perform the prebattle sacrifice to send the soldiers into war more confidently, was a stinging one: "Hath the Lord as great delight in burnt offerings and sacrifices, as in obeying the voice of the Lord? Behold, to obey is better than sacrifice, and to hearken than the fat of rams." (1 Sam. 15:22.)

As Israel's prophet, Samuel also chose David to suc-

131

ceed Saul. David was an idealistic, beloved, and honored king, a charismatic leader, and a brilliant military strategist who brought Israel to her greatest moment. However, his power corrupted his sense of values. He thought that as king he could do as he pleased. When he desired Bathsheba, he seduced her. When she became pregnant with his child, David issued orders that placed her husband, Uriah, at the forefront of the battle, where he was killed. David then married the widow.

But another prophet, Nathan, confronted David in his sins by relating to him a trenchant parable:

> There were two men in one city; the one rich, and the other poor.
>
> The rich man had exceeding many flocks and herds:
>
> But the poor man had nothing, save one little ewe lamb, which he had bought and nourished up: and it grew up together with him, and with his children; it did eat of his own meat, and drank of his own cup, and lay in his bosom, and was unto him as a daughter.
>
> And there came a traveller unto the rich man, and he spared to take of his own flock and of his own herd, to dress for the wayfaring man that was come unto him; but took the poor man's lamb, and dressed it for the man that was come to him.
>
> And David's anger was greatly kindled against the man; and he said to Nathan, As the Lord liveth, the man that hath done this thing shall surely die:
>
> And he shall restore the lamb fourfold, because he did this thing, and because he had no pity.
>
> And Nathan said to David, Thou art the man. Thus saith the Lord God of Israel, I anointed thee king over Israel, and I delivered thee out of the hand of Saul;
>
> And I gave thee thy master's house, and thy master's wives into thy bosom, and gave thee the house of Israel and of Judah; and if that had been too little, I would moreover have given unto thee such and such things.
>
> Wherefore hast thou despised the commandment of the Lord, to do evil in his sight? thou hast killed Uriah the Hittite

with the sword, and hast taken his wife to be thy wife, and hast slain him with the sword of the children of Ammon.

Now therefore the sword shall never depart from thine house; because thou hast despised me, and hast taken the wife of Uriah the Hittite to be thy wife.

Thus saith the Lord, Behold, I will raise up evil against thee out of thine own house, and I will take thy wives before thine eyes, and give them unto thy neighbour, and he shall lie with thy wives in the sight of this sun.

For thou didst it secretly: but I will do this thing before all Israel, and before the sun. (2 Sam. 12:1-12.)

Another dramatic illustration of God's righteous will being superior to that of the king's is the story of the prophet Elijah and Ahab, king of Israel. Ahab wished to enlarge his palatial estate by annexing Naboth's vineyard. Naboth refused to sell his land because he would be untrue to his heritage—his inheritance in Israel. As Ahab lay on his bed, sulking like a child, his foreign wife, Jezebel, took the situation in charge and said to him: "Dost thou now govern the kingdom of Israel? arise, and eat bread, and let thine heart be merry: I will give thee the vineyard of Naboth the Jezreelite." (1 Kings 21:7.)

Jezebel had Naboth falsely accused of blaspheming God and the king. After Naboth was stoned to death, Jezebel told Ahab: "Arise, take possession of the vineyard of Naboth . . . for Naboth is not alive, but dead." (1 Kgs. 21:15.)

Such a solution is fully in the tradition of absolute monarchies, but in Israel, kings were not beyond criticism and a higher judgment:

And the word of the Lord came to Elijah the Tishbite, saying,

Arise, go down to meet Ahab king of Israel, which is in Samaria: behold, he is in the vineyard of Naboth, whither he is gone down to possess it.

And thou shalt speak unto him, saying, Thus saith the Lord, Hast thou killed, and also taken possession? And thou shalt speak unto him, saying, Thus saith the Lord, In the place where dogs licked the blood of Naboth shall dogs lick thy blood, even thine.

And Ahab said to Elijah, Hast thou found me, O mine enemy? And he answered, I have found thee: because thou hast sold thyself to work evil in the sight of the Lord.

Behold, I will bring evil upon thee, and will take away thy posterity. . . .

And of Jezebel also spake the Lord, saying, The dogs shall eat Jezebel by the wall of Jezreel. (1 Kgs. 21:17-21, 23.)

The writing prophets, particularly Micah, Isaiah, and Jeremiah, continued to monitor and chastise princes and kings of Israel. People in high places — perhaps especially people in high places — were still subject to a higher power. The will of God took precedence over the rights of kings. About 730 B.C., Micah attacked the power structure of Israel:

And I said, Hear, I pray you, O heads of Jacob, and ye princes of the house of Israel; Is it not for you to know judgment?

Who hate the good, and love the evil; who pluck off their skin from off them, and their flesh from off their bones;

Who also eat the flesh of my people, and flay their skin from off them; and they break their bones, and chop them in pieces, as for the pot, and as flesh within the caldron.

Then shall they cry unto the Lord, but he will not hear them: he will even hide his face from them at that time, as they have behaved themselves ill in their doings.

Thus saith the Lord concerning the prophets that make my people err, that bite with their teeth, and cry, Peace; and he that putteth not into their mouths, they even prepare war against him.

Therefore night shall be unto you, that ye shall not have a vision; and it shall be dark unto you, that ye shall not divine; and the sun shall go down over the prophets, and the day shall be dark over them.

Then shall the seers be ashamed, and the diviners confounded: yea, they shall all cover their lips; for there is no answer of God.

But truly I am full of power by the spirit of the Lord, and of judgment, and of might, to declare unto Jacob his transgression, and to Israel his sin.

Hear this, I pray you, ye heads of the house of Jacob, and princes of the house of Israel, that abhor judgment, and pervert all equity,

They build up Zion with blood, and Jerusalem with iniquity.

The heads thereof judge for reward, and the priests thereof teach for hire, and the prophets thereof divine for money: yet will they lean upon the Lord, and say, Is not the Lord among us? none evil can come upon us.

Therefore shall Zion for your sake be plowed as a field, and Jerusalem shall become heaps, and the mountain of the house as the high places of the forest. (Micah 3:1-12.)

The later chapters of Isaiah eloquently proclaim the power of God and the comparative insignificance of earthly kingdoms:

Who hath directed the Spirit of the Lord, or being his counsellor hath taught him?

With whom took he counsel, and who instructed him, and taught him in the path of judgment, and taught him knowledge, and shewed to him the way of understanding?

Behold, the nations are as a drop of a bucket, and are counted as the small dust of the balance: behold, he taketh up the isles as a very little thing. (Isa. 40:13-15.)

For centuries, people have struggled to gain political freedom and to limit the power of autocratic rulers. England has led the way in modern times, beginning with the Magna Carta in A.D. 1215. The American Revolutionary War and the French Revolution reveal the high price people have been willing to pay to rid themselves of monarchial power.

What power the Old Testament may have had in such events by supplying a precedent of God as the ultimate authority! And would that all men and women with power and influence would respect a moral order in the universe as the Old Testament prophets did!

Chapter 20
A COVENANT PEOPLE

The Old Testament reveals a new and remarkable relationship between the Lord and Israel, a relationship that, in its turn, becomes the structural foundation for the rest of the events of the Old Testament.

It all began with a call to Abraham to leave his native country and establish his posterity as a new people, a separate nation who would become a blessing to all people:

> Now the Lord had said unto Abram, Get thee out of thy country, and from thy kindred, and from thy father's house, unto a land that I will show thee:
> And I will make of thee a great nation, and I will bless thee, and make thy name great; and thou shalt be a blessing:
> And I will bless them that bless thee, and curse him that curseth thee: and in thee shall all families of the earth be blessed. (Gen. 12:1-3.)

A covenant is an agreement between parties, each committed to perform certain things on behalf of the other. In this instance, the Israelites accepted the obligation to obey God, keep his commandments, and be a blessing to all the families of the world. God in turn bound himself to prosper them, prolong their lives, preserve their country, and call them his very own. In Hosea, God calls his relationship to Israel a marriage, he being a husband.

For the sake of Abraham, God renewed the covenant with Isaac:

> And the Lord appeared unto him, and said, Go not down into Egypt; dwell in the land which I shall tell thee of:
>
> Sojourn in this land, and I will be with thee, and will bless thee; for unto thee, and unto thy seed, I will give all these countries, and I will perform the oath which I sware unto Abraham thy father;
>
> And I will make thy seed to multiply as the stars of heaven, and will give unto thy seed all these countries; and in thy seed shall all the nations of the earth be blessed;
>
> Because that Abraham obeyed my voice, and kept my charge, my commandments, my statutes, and my laws. (Gen. 26:2-5.)

God also covenanted with Jacob:

> And [Jacob] dreamed, and behold a ladder set up on the earth, and the top of it reached to heaven: and behold the angels of God ascending and descending on it.
>
> And, behold, the Lord stood above it, and said, I am the Lord God of Abraham thy father, and the God of Isaac: the land whereon thou liest, to thee will I give it, and to thy seed;
>
> And thy seed shall be as the dust of the earth, and thou shalt spread abroad to the west, and to the east, and to the north, and to the south: and in thee and in thy seed shall all the families of the earth be blessed.
>
> And, behold, I am with thee, and will keep thee in all places whither thou goest, and will bring thee again into this land; for I will not leave thee, until I have done that which I have spoken to thee of (Gen. 28:12-15.)
>
> And God said unto him, Thy name is Jacob: thy name shall not be called any more Jacob, but Israel shall be thy name: and he called his name Israel.
>
> And God said unto him, I am God Almighty: be fruitful

and multiply; a nation and a company of nations shall be of thee, and kings shall come out of thy loins;

And the land which I gave Abraham and Isaac, to thee I will give it, and to thy seed after thee will I give the land. (35:10-12.)

Great promises were made to Joseph:

Joseph is a fruitful bough, even a fruitful bough by a well; whose branches run over the wall:

The archers have sorely grieved him, and shot at him, and hated him:

But his bow abode in strength, and the arms of his hands were made strong by the hands of the mighty God of Jacob; (from thence is the shepherd, the stone of Israel:)

Even by the God of thy father, who shall help thee; and by the Almighty, who shall bless thee with blessings of heaven above, blessings of the deep that lieth under, blessings of the breasts, and of the womb:

The blessings of thy father have prevailed above the blessings of my progenitors unto the utmost bound of the everlasting hills: they shall be on the head of Joseph, and on the crown of the head of him that was separate from his brethren. (Gen. 49:22-26.)

Before the Israelites entered the land of Canaan, Moses renewed the covenant between his people and the Lord:

And Moses called all Israel, and said unto them, Hear, O Israel, the statutes and judgments which I speak in your ears this day, that ye may learn them, and keep, and do them.

The Lord our God made a covenant with us in Horeb.

The Lord made not this covenant with our fathers, but with us, even us, who are all of us here alive this day. (Deut. 5:1-3.)

In beautiful, earnest language, Moses states the people's relationship to God. This passage has been read in Jewish synagogues every sabbath for centuries:

Hear therefore, O Israel, and observe to do it; that it may

be well with thee, and that ye may increase mightily, as the
Lord God of thy fathers hath promised thee, in the land that
floweth with milk and honey.

Hear, O Israel: The Lord our God is one Lord:

And thou shalt love the Lord thy God with all thine heart,
and with all thy soul, and with all thy might.

And these words, which I command thee this day, shall
be in thine heart:

And thou shalt teach them diligently unto thy children,
and shalt talk of them when thou sittest in thine house, and
when thou walkest by the way, and when thou liest down,
and when thou risest up.

And thou shalt bind them for a sign upon thine hand,
and they shall be as frontlets between thine eyes.

And thou shalt write them upon the posts of thy house,
and on thy gates. (Deut. 6:3-9.)

These scriptures represent something deeply satisfying to the human soul. It is part of our nature to seek
a connection with the divine. We yearn to know and be
known by our Creator. A covenant is a reciprocal relationship, one that God offers to men and women, and
his own invitation to us to enter into a relationship of
promise and sanctification with him. In a world that is
always changing and often threatening, such a covenant
offers us security, a point of permanence, a promise that
we will be cherished and nurtured through life's vicis-
situdes.

However, if the desire for such a covenant relationship speaks to the deepest roots of human nature, the
clearest lessons of human history are that such a covenant is desperately difficult to keep. There is plenty of
evidence that Israel and Judah, with the exception of a
few prophets and possibly their disciples, were not true
to their covenants. They practiced neither justice nor
mercy. They served God with burnt offerings, rituals,
and feasts, but not with purity of heart. Israel, the northern kingdom, fell to Assyria in 721 B.C. and Judah to

Babylon in 586 B.C. as the prophets predicted. Israel had forfeited the protection of the Lord through unrighteousness.

The Israelites misinterpreted what it means to be a chosen people. They thought it meant power, favors, and privileges, not duties and responsibilities. I am not sure, however, that they failed completely. By their mere existence, sinful and wayward though they were, they reminded the nations of the earth of the existence of God, were a living lesson in faith even in their infidelity, and were a constant reminder of the steadfastness of God's covenant. I wonder if Abraham saw the tangled and ambiguous history of his descendants when he swore that first oath and covenant. I wonder if he hoped to help God establish a people who could fulfill the Lord's purposes in human history.

As we have already noted, the author of Jonah spoke strongly against the egocentric and shortsighted idea of Israel that gospel principles applied only to them. The later chapters of Isaiah describe Israel's calling in other words, as God's servant to be a light to the Gentiles:

> I the Lord have called thee in righteousness, and will hold thine hand, and will keep thee, and give thee for a covenant of the people, for a light of the Gentiles;
> To open the blind eyes, to bring out the prisoners from the prison, and them that sit in darkness out of the prison house. (Isa. 42:6-7.)
> Behold, I have refined thee, but not with silver; I have chosen thee in the furnace of affliction. (Isa. 48:10.)
> And said unto me, Thou art my servant, O Israel, in whom I will be glorified. . . .
> And he said, It is a light thing that thou shouldest be my servant to raise up the tribes of Jacob, and to restore the preserved of Israel: I will also give thee for a light to the Gentiles, that thou mayest be my salvation unto the end of the earth. (Isa. 49:3, 6.)
> Arise, shine; for thy light is come, and the glory of the Lord is risen upon thee.

> For, behold, the darkness shall cover the earth, and gross darkness the people: but the Lord shall arise upon thee, and his glory shall be seen upon thee.
>
> And the Gentiles shall come to thy light, and kings to the brightness of thy rising. (Isa. 60:1-3.)
>
> Ye are my witnesses, saith the Lord, and my servant whom I have chosen: that ye may know and believe me, and understand that I am he: before me there was no God formed, neither shall there be after me. (Isa. 43:10.)

The prophets of Israel came to understand Israel's true mission of a covenant people of the Lord. They conclude their writing in the faith that the Lord will redeem Israel, despite her backslidings, because he is a merciful God who honors the promises made to Father Abraham. The covenant rests not only upon the faithful past of Father Abraham but upon the expectation of salvation of every believing member of the house of Israel. It is a present claim upon the living God, who is a merciful God, that keeps the covenant alive in every heart:

> Who is a God like unto thee, that pardoneth iniquity, and passeth by the transgression of the remnant of his heritage? he retaineth not his anger for ever, because he delighteth in mercy.
>
> He will turn again, he will have compassion upon us; he will subdue our iniquities; and thou wilt cast all their sins into the depths of the sea.
>
> Thou wilt perform the truth to Jacob, and the mercy to Abraham, which thou hast sworn unto our fathers from the days of old. (Micah 7:18-20.)
>
> For Zion's sake will I not hold my peace, and for Jerusalem's sake I will not rest, until the righteousness thereof go forth as brightness, and the salvation thereof as a lamp that burneth.
>
> And the Gentiles shall see thy righteousness, and all kings thy glory: and thou shalt be called by a new name, which the mouth of the Lord shall name.
>
> Thou shalt also be a crown of glory in the hand of the Lord, and a royal diadem in the hand of thy God.

142

Thou shalt no more be termed Forsaken; neither shall thy land any more be termed Desolate: but thou shalt be called Hephzi-bah, and thy land Beulah: for the Lord delighteth in thee. . . .The Lord hath sworn by his right hand, and by the arm of his strength, Surely I will no more give thy corn to be meat for thine enemies; and the sons of the stranger shall not drink thy wine, for the which thou hast laboured:

But they that have gathered it shall eat it, and praise the Lord; and they that have brought it together shall drink it in the courts of my holiness.

Go through, go through the gates; prepare ye the way of the people; cast up, cast up the highway; gather out the stones; lift up a standard for the people.

Behold, the Lord hath proclaimed unto the end of the world, Say ye to the daughter of Zion, Behold, thy salvation cometh; behold, his reward is with him, and his work before him.

And they shall call them, The holy people, The redeemed of the Lord. (Isa. 62:1-4, 8-12.)

Latter-day Saints call themselves modern Israel. Patriarchal blessings declare them to be descendants of Joseph through Ephraim and Manasseh. We are also a covenant people, called to fulfill the mission that ancient Israel and the Nephites failed to realize. God needs a people who will lead the rest of humankind to faith in God and his righteousness as taught by the Hebrew prophets and Jesus.

Heaven forbid that we think ourselves better than other peoples. May we rather believe that we were chosen to fulfill a mission by demonstrating what it means to serve God and do his will. May we, in the words of Micah, do what the Lord requires of us: "to do justly, and to love mercy, and to walk humbly with [our] God." (Micah 6:8.)

Chapter 21

THE VISION OF PEACE:
SWORDS INTO PLOWSHARES

The history of the Near East in Old Testament times is a round of repeated warfare between Israel and her neighbors, including the great empires of the Nile and Mesopotamia. Canaan, caught in the middle both politically and geographically, found itself under the actual or potential domination of Egypt, Assyria, Babylonia, Persia, and later Greece and Rome. As the prophets had predicted, both Israel and Judah went into captivity, and their people were scattered among the nations.

Since biblical days, we have done no better. The inspiring restoration of the modern nation of Israel to its ancient homeland has taken place in a context no less threatening than that facing Moses' people in the first conquest of Canaan. A challenging presence in the Middle East, Israel has defended itself from annihilation repeatedly in the short decades since its reestablishment in 1948, its very presence disturbing to its hostile neighbors.

Elsewhere on our globe, constant warfare has been the burden and tragedy of humankind. And it is still with us — but now with the threat of total annihilation.

145

It is encouraging and inspiring that the prophets, despite their terrifying understanding of the destruction that awaited disobedient human beings, also had a vision of a golden age of peace. Both Micah and Isaiah make this promise in the same words, suggesting that one may have borrowed from the other:

> But in the last days it shall come to pass, that the mountain of the house of the Lord shall be established in the top of the mountains, and it shall be exalted above the hills; and people shall flow unto it.
>
> And many nations shall come, and say, Come, and let us go up to the mountain of the Lord, and to the house of the God of Jacob; and he will teach us of his ways, and we will walk in his paths: for the law shall go forth of Zion, and the word of the Lord from Jerusalem.
>
> And he shall judge among many people, and rebuke strong nations afar off; and they shall beat their swords into plowshares, and their spears into pruninghooks: nation shall not lift up a sword against nation, neither shall they learn war any more.
>
> But they shall sit every man under his vine and under his fig tree; and none shall make them afraid: for the mouth of the Lord of hosts hath spoken it.
>
> For all people will walk every one in the name of his god, and we will walk in the name of the Lord our God for ever and ever. (Micah 4:1-5; see also Isa. 2:1-4.)

In contemporary life, these beautiful words mean that we can spend less for armaments and more for health care, shelter for the homeless, food for the hungry, education, arts, and research. Who would not pray the Lord to hasten the day of fulfillment?

Despite our concerns for living well in the present and honoring worthy past achievements, we must also look forward in faith and hope to a great future. The redemption of Israel and the establishment of peace will be achieved with the coming of a Messiah. In this belief, we can sense close affinity with our Old Testament kin-

146

folk in spirit. For Christians, this Messiah will be Jesus Christ, returning a second time to the earth. In addition to the Old Testament passages interpreted in the New Testament as predictions of Christ's coming, Latter-day Saints have corroborating passages in The Book of Mormon and in the book of Moses in the Pearl of Great Price. (See James E. Talmage, *Jesus the Christ*, ch. 5.)

However, if we scrutinize the Old Testament by itself, without reference to other scriptures, we observe that Christ is not named and we do not gain a clear picture of the nature of the Messiah. Because the Jews were dominated by their larger neighbors, they quite naturally looked for a temporal savior in the image of a King David. But the prophets, particularly Isaiah and Micah, had intimations of a spiritual Messiah. Christ's coming fulfills many of their expectations:

> Now gather thyself in troops, O daughter of troops: he hath laid siege against us: they shall smite the judge of Israel with a rod upon the cheek.
> But thou, Bethlehem Ephratah, though thou be little among the thousands of Judah, yet out of thee shall he come forth unto me that is to be ruler in Israel; whose goings forth have been from of old, from everlasting. (Micah 5:1-2.)

A clear reference to a spiritual Messiah is found in Isaiah:

> For unto us a child is born, unto us a son is given: and the government shall be upon his shoulder: and his name shall be called Wonderful, Counsellor, The mighty God, The everlasting Father, The Prince of peace.
> Of the increase of his government and peace there shall be no end, upon the throne of David, and upon his kingdom, to order it, and to establish it with judgment and with justice from henceforth even for ever. The zeal of the Lord of hosts will perform this. (Isa. 9:6-7.)

Jesus Christ fulfills this passage admirably.

The tone of Isaiah changes radically from chapter 40

on—to such an extent that scholars speak of Deutero-Isaiah, or second Isaiah. The setting for these chapters is the Jewish captivity in Babylon.

Isaiah 53 describes the humiliation and suffering of God's servant on behalf of others. Some scholars think this passage describes the role of Israel. Christian students see in it a very detailed and specific anticipation of the mission, life, and death of Jesus Christ. The gospel accounts fulfill this chapter of Isaiah faithfully:

Who hath believed our report? and to whom is the arm of the Lord revealed?

For he shall grow up before him as a tender plant, and as a root out of a dry ground: he hath no form nor comeliness; and when we shall see him, there is no beauty that we should desire him.

He is despised and rejected of men; a man of sorrows, and acquainted with grief: and we hid as it were our faces from him; he was despised, and we esteemed him not.

Surely he hath borne our griefs, and carried our sorrows: yet we did esteem him stricken, smitten of God, and afflicted.

But he was wounded for our transgressions, he was bruised for our iniquities: the chastisement of our peace was upon him; and with his stripes we are healed.

All we like sheep have gone astray; we have turned every one to his own way; and the Lord hath laid on him the iniquity of us all.

He was oppressed, and he was afflicted, yet he opened not his mouth: he is brought as a lamb to the slaughter, and as a sheep before her shearers is dumb, so he openeth not his mouth.

He was taken from prison and from judgment: and who shall declare his generation: for he was cut off out of the land of the living: for the transgression of my people was he stricken.

And he made his grave with the wicked, and with the rich in his death; because he had done no violence, neither was any deceit in his mouth.

Yet it pleased the Lord to bruise him; he hath put him to grief: when thou shalt make his soul an offering for sin, he shall see his seed, he shall prolong his days, and the pleasure of the Lord shall prosper in his hand.

He shall see of the travail of his soul, and shall be satisfied: by his knowledge shall my righteous servant justify many; for he shall bear their iniquities.

Therefore will I divide him a portion with the great and he shall divide the spoil with the strong because he hath poured out his soul unto death: and he was numbered with the transgressors; and he bare the sin of many, and made intercession for the transgressors. (Isa. 53:1-12.)

EPILOGUE

We come to the end of this Old Testament review, very much aware that we have barely touched upon the many important concepts in this rich, ancient record. Nor have we considered many books of the Old Testament as such. My purpose has been to reveal some basic, significant ideas that occur in many of the books.

Not all of the Old Testament is of one quality. Much of it bears witness to a God of truth and righteousness who made known his will to his servants, the prophets and prophetesses of Israel. Some of the writings by unknown, well-intentioned authors reflect a limited understanding of Deity. We can learn from the errors and sins of Israel as well as from their religious and ethical insights. To discern the meaning and truth of scripture, we need to bring to our study humility, a knowledge of the great fundamentals of religion, the emphasis of Jesus (for Christians), and the influence of the Holy Spirit.

With the help of a Bible commentary and the appendixes, you will be able to study the individual books with interest and, I hope, greater insight and understanding. The ideas still relevant to our religious living today connect us with the eternal themes of the gospel and with those who have, with faith and hope, sought the ways of the Lord before us.

What are some of the most important teachings of the Old Testament? I find them in the perception the prophets arrived at concerning God and his relationship to human beings. God is an ethical being, a person of integrity and compassion, deeply committed to the well-being of his children, who have been created in his image and likeness. Because we are in the divine image, we too must be just and merciful.

A second important concept is that there is a moral order in the universe. Ethical laws govern the lives of human beings. There can be no prosperity, no well-being, no peace in the life of an individual, a nation, or the world until people learn to practice justice and mercy. Rituals, holy days, and sacred beliefs are a means to an end — not to be worshipped in themselves but of value as they draw us nearer to God and to our fellow human beings.

Our Christian faith and living can be enormously strengthened by the Old Testament concepts of ethical monotheism and by the concrete and specific illustrations of proper human relationships in the law of Moses.

Until we learn to hold human life — every human life — sacred, we shall not have peace on earth. Peace presupposes "good will toward men." (Luke 2:14.) Both the Old Testament and our Christian faith challenge us to put human values — the well-being of all people — above material values and even above our own interests. Jesus said, "He that findeth his life shall lose it: and he that loseth his life for my sake shall find it." (Matt. 10:39.) Jesus, like the prophets before him, was concerned with people — the sick and the afflicted, the poor, sinners, publicans, the alienated of society. So were Moses, Isaiah, and Micah. Are we?

Proverbs, Ecclesiastes, and Job are eloquently and

beautifully written, containing much practical wisdom. They merit our reflection and meditation.

Psalms inspire and encourage us to worship God in "the beauty of holiness."

Characters of the Old Testament portray both the virtues and the follies of human beings. Vicariously, they teach us of the good and evil mingled in all human experience.

All in all, the Old Testament is a unique and priceless record, Israel's religious interpretation of life and history.

THE BOOKS OF THE OLD TESTAMENT

I. THE LAW (PENTATEUCH, TORAH)

1. *Genesis.* Describes the creation; tells of Cain and Abel, Noah and the flood; portrays in considerable detail the lives of the great forebears of Israel: Abraham and Sarah, Isaac and Rebekah, Jacob, Rachel and Leah, and Joseph.
2. *Exodus.* Relates the call of Moses to lead Israel out of Egyptian bondage and how it was done; contains the Decalogue (Ten Commandments); is an interesting study of the character of Moses and his relationship to God and his people.
3. *Numbers.* Continues the account in Exodus; describes life in the wilderness on the way to Canaan; contains the Lord's blessing upon the children of Israel ("The Lord bless thee, and keep thee: the Lord make his face shine upon thee"—Num. 6:23-27).
4. *Leviticus.* Contains a description of much of the ritual life of Israel: sacrifices, things clean and unclean, and so forth. Chapters 19 and 25 contain some fine ethical-religious teachings.
5. *Deuteronomy.* Contains the most complete and finest statement of specific Mosaic laws; given as an

oration by Moses before Israel entered the land of Canaan, mingling both warning and promise.

II. THE FORMER PROPHETS, HISTORICAL BOOKS

6. *Joshua.* Tells of Joshua's role as leader in replacing Moses and of his conquest of Canaan and the distribution of the land among the tribes; Joshua praised for his faithfulness.
7. *Judges.* Covers the period between Joshua and Samuel; relates the exploits of such heroes as Deborah, Gideon, and Samson. Not a religiously inspiring book.
8. *1 Samuel.* Contains the call and mission of the prophet Samuel, the rise and fall of Saul, and David's relationship to Saul.
9. *2 Samuel.* Records David's glorious and tragic reign.
10. *1 Kings.* Records Solomon's reign, the division of the kingdom at his death, and the couragous mission of Elijah.
11. *2 Kings.* Records the fall of Israel to Assyria in 722 B.C. and the fall of Judah to Babylon in 586 B.C. Age of the great writing prophets: Amos, Hosea, Micah, Isaiah, Jeremiah, and Ezekiel.

III. THE LATER PROPHETS

12. *Amos* (ca. 760-740 B.C.). Records the mission of Amos, shepherd from the kingdom of Judah, to northern Israel (Bethel); he condemns Israel for its lack of social morality and predicts its captivity; powerful message of justice.
13. *Hosea* (ca. 745-735 B.C.). Describes the faithfulness of Israel to God in terms of his own faithless wife; predicts the captivity and ultimate redemption of Israel.
14. *Micah* (ca. 730-720 B.C.). Records the mission of a villager from Judea who condemns the materialistic

and uncompassionate life of Jerusalem and attacks the political and ecclesiastical framework; defines true religion (Micah 6:6-8).

15. *Isaiah* (ca. 740-700 B.C.). Describes the mission of an aristocratic advisor to the kings of Judah who expresses great trust in God through righteous living and (from chapter 40 on) predicts the divine triumph on behalf of Israel.

16. *Jeremiah* (ca. 621-586 B.C.). Describes the mission of the last great prophet before the fall of Judah, who predicted the coming captivity in Babylon and tried to prepare his people for it; insisted on purity and righteousness.

17. *Ezekiel* (ca. 592-567 B.C.). Records the mission of this prophet to Israel in Babylonian captivity; makes a transition from national to individual emphasis in religion. See Chapter 18.

18. *Zephaniah* (ca. 627 B.C.). Records his warning that divine wrath is about to be poured out on Judah, Jerusalem, and all unbelievers; a remnant will eventually be saved.

19. *Nahum* (ca. 612 B.C.). Contains a powerful, poetic prediction of the fall of proud, wicked Nineveh; pleads with Judah to trust in the Lord.

20. *Habakkuk* (ca. 608-597 B.C.). Portrays the prophet's despair over the fall of Judah and Jerusalem but ends on a note of triumphant trust in and loyalty to God.

21. *Haggai* (ca. 520-519 B.C.). Records the prophet's mission to Judah after the return from the Babylonian exile; urges the people to rebuild the temple.

22. *Zechariah* (ca. 520-519 B.C.). Contains a prophetic vision of the restoration of Jerusalem and the triumph of God on Israel's behalf.

23. *Obadiah* (ca. 460-450 B.C.). Gives a brief prediction of the destruction of Edom for its persecution of Israel.

24. *Joel* (ca. 400 B.C.). Contains prediction of a locust plague as a forerunner to the coming of the day of the Lord.
25. *Malachi* (ca. 400 B.C.). Contains instructions from the Lord to obey, pay tithing; tells of the mission of Elijah.
26. *Jonah* (ca. 350 B.C.). Records a classic story teaching the impartiality, mercy, and universality of God.

IV. THE WRITINGS

27. *Proverbs.* Records the wisdom of centuries in a collection of proverbs and admonishments to Israel; positive, affirmative, motivational, and practical.
28. *Ecclesiastes.* Gives an eloquent appraisal of life from late in the history of Israel — realistic and even pessimistic in tone.
29. *Job.* Contains a dramatic, poetic debate focusing on explanations of human suffering in a world created by God; a classic in religious thought and literary form.
30. *Psalms.* Presents a collection of songs of praise sung in Israel over the centuries.
31. *Ruth.* Records the idyll of a Moabite woman who accompanies her beloved mother-in-law to Israel, marries Boaz, and becomes the great-grandmother of King David; teaches tolerance for the non-Jew.
32. *Esther.* Contains the narrative of a Jewish woman who becomes queen of Persia and saves her people from destruction at the hands of a jealous minister; historical accuracy uncertain.
33. *Ezra* (ca. 520 B.C.). Records the mission of a religious leader who restored the Israelite religion when the exiles returned to Judah; asked Israelite men to abandon Gentile wives.
34. *Nehemiah* (ca. 465-424 B.C.). Continues the ac-

count in Ezra from the perspective of a secular leader; Nehemiah rebuilds the walls of Jerusalem.

35. *Lamentations.* Records mourning over the fall of Jerusalem; ascribed to Jeremiah.

36. *Daniel.* Contains a heroic account of the triumphs of Daniel and associates in captivity; gives hope to Israel at a difficult time in its history.

37. *The Song of Solomon.* Preserves a Hebrew love poem.

38-39. *1 and 2 Chronicles.* Covers history from the creation of the world to the fall of Jerusalem, with heavier emphasis on the events in the kingdom of Judah; overlaps the prophetic books; author unknown but probably written after the Babylonian captivity.

EPIC STORIES FROM GENESIS

The book of Genesis contains foundation stories, narratives that explain how the world came to be as it is and who the founders were. These narratives gave the house of Israel — and all Judeo-Christian adherents after them — a framework for understanding how things fit together into a world purposefully created by God for the benefit of his prime creations, human beings. It also assured the Israelites that their nation was established by Abraham, Isaac, Jacob, and Joseph — men blessed of God to establish the people of Israel.

The creation is described in simple, meaningful language that a child can understand. Relatively free of obvious mythology, it is a profoundly religious statement declaring that God was the author of creation and that creation was good because it was purposeful. Noteworthy is the final statement that human beings, male and female, were created in the image of God and that this creation was *very* good. This account of creation was written by a nonscientific author before a scientific worldview existed. Therefore, to read it as though it were a textbook in geology, astronomy, or any other science would be an inappropriate use of the text. Its purpose is religious: to glorify God as the creator of the earth and all of its life forms, including human beings. Humans have a special relationship with God by being created in his image and also a special responsibility by being given dominion over the earth and its animals.

Following the creation stories comes the important story of Cain and Abel (Genesis 4). After Cain killed his brother Abel, the Lord called him to account. Cain asked, "Am I my brother's keeper?" The obvious answer was yes; and the principle of interrelationship and concern with treating other persons ethically was reiterated in the law of Moses and in the writings of the prophets. People have social responsibilities and must be benevolently concerned with the welfare of their fellow creatures.

That is the first important principle to be learned from this narrative. The second is that there is no place for vengeance in punishments for crime. God set his mark on Cain so that no one, meeting him, would take justice into his or her own hands and slay this first murderer. Punishment belongs to society. The offended party cannot be trusted to mete out justice. I think it is particularly important to remember that God set that mark on Cain, not as a curse but as a protection.

The next important narrative is that of Noah and the flood (Gen. 6–10). Some aspects of the flood story are hard to believe in detail. How could Noah literally catch, house, and feed two animals of every species? How could he, without experience, construct a seaworthy craft of that size? But these details need not concern us, nor need the question of whether the flood literally covered the globe or whether it simply inundated the lands that Noah knew. We simply need to understand that there was a cataclysmic flood. The important religious message of this story is the teaching that moral law prevails in the universe. Individuals or peoples who ignore or otherwise transgress basic ethical principles cause profound disharmonies with universal moral law. This wrongness demands redress, and the process of that redressing can cause immense destruction.

Most of the remainder of Genesis (aside from several genealogies) is a series of fascinating stories about the patriarchs and matriarchs of Israel who were called and blessed of God with great promises for their posterity. Here we learn of Abraham and Sarah, Isaac and Rebekah, Jacob and Rachel and Leah, and Joseph and Asenath.

Abraham and Sarah, father and mother of the Hebrews, are honored as the source and fountainhead of the house of Israel. Both were individuals of great faith. Their first act of faith was to leave their home country, go to a strange land, and live among unknown people who would not likely welcome their coming. It is significant that Sarah was a partner in this process, even though the initial revelations came to Abraham and he was almost certainly the person who initiated the action.

An unusual incident illustrating the generosity of Abraham is recorded in Genesis 13. His nephew Lot accompanied him into the land of promise. Each had flocks and herds, too many for the available pasture. Generously, Abraham offered Lot his choice of lands to eliminate the conflict between Abraham's herdsmen and Lot's, not to mention the local people. Abraham explained his offer: "Let there be no strife, I pray thee, between me and thee . . . for we be brethren." (Gen. 13:8.) Lot observed the "plain of Jordan, that it was well watered every where, before the Lord destroyed Sodom and Gomorrah, even as the garden of the Lord." (Gen. 13:10.) Lot made his choice and went to the plain of Jordan, clearly the better land, while Abraham dwelt in the land of Canaan. Lot's choice created difficulty with his neighbors and exposed him to capture. Instead of saying, "I told you so," Abraham promptly mobilized his servants and freed

Lot, restoring his possessions and, more importantly, maintaining their relationship intact.

It was a great joy to both Abraham and Sarah when the Lord fulfilled his promise to make Abraham a "nation" and Sarah gave birth to her only child, Isaac. The ultimate test of faith for Abraham was his belief that he must sacrifice his only son to God. No mention is made of Sarah's role in this event. Perhaps she did not know it was occurring, or surely she would have intervened in some way. It is impossible for me to believe that a mother who had experienced God as tender, protective, and responsive to her patient prayers would have acquiesced in such a demand. It is also difficult to believe that God would test a man's faith by asking him to violate not only a clear commandment but also the deepest human feelings that he possessed (see Micah 6:6-8). I doubt that we have the whole story of this incident.

When Isaac became of marriageable age, Abraham sent a trusted servant back to Abraham's people to find him a wife. The servant used good judgment, as well as faith, to carry out his mission and find Rebekah. The story introduces romance into the Bible, even though Rebekah and Isaac eventually fomented strife between their sons, Esau and Jacob, through blatant favoritism.

Jacob's love for Rachel is a second romantic tale in Genesis that has important consequences for the children. Jacob's clear favoritism for Rachel's two sons, to the exclusion of his other ten sons by Leah and the two concubines, caused them to hate Joseph, sell him as a slave, and eventually meet him in Egypt as second in importance only to the pharaoh—a dazzling tale.

The story of Joseph is a moving account. His life anticipates, in some respects, the history and fate of Israel. Joseph rose from slavery to be administrator of Egypt. He was honorable in an hour of temptation. He saved his family in the day of famine and found a home for them in the land of Goshen, where they were eventually enslaved by a pharaoh who did not know Joseph. A very eloquent and emotional part of the story is the plea of his brother Judah for Joseph to let him remain a servant but to permit another brother, young Benjamin, to return to their aged father:

> Then Judah came near unto him, and said, O my lord, let thy servant, I pray thee, speak a word in my lord's ears, and let not thine anger burn against thy servant: for thou art even as Pharaoh.
>
> My lord asked his servants, saying, Have ye a father, or a brother?
>
> And we said unto my lord, We have a father, an old man, and a child of his old age, a little one; and his brother is dead, and he alone is left of his mother, and his father loveth him.
>
> And thou saidst unto thy servants, Bring him down unto me, that I may set mine eyes upon him.
>
> And we said unto my lord, The lad cannot leave his father: or if he should leave his father, his father would die.
>
> And thou saidst unto thy servants, Except your youngest brother come down with you, ye shall see my face no more.
>
> And it came to pass when we came up unto thy servant my father, we told him the words of my lord.
>
> And our father said, Go again, and buy us a little food.
>
> And we said, We cannot go down: if our youngest brother be with us, then will we go down: for we may not see the man's face, except our youngest brother be with us.
>
> And thy servant my father said unto us, Ye know that my wife bare me two sons:
>
> And the one went out from me, and I said, Surely he is torn in pieces; and I saw him not since:
>
> And if ye take this also from me, and mischief befall him, ye shall bring down my gray hairs with sorrow to the grave.
>
> Now therefore when I come to thy servant my father, and the lad be not with us; seeing that his life is bound up in the lad's life;
>
> It shall come to pass, when he seeth that the lad is not with us, that he will die: and thy servants shall bring down

the gray hairs of thy servant our father with sorrow to the grave.

For thy servant became surety for the lad unto my father, saying, If I bring him not unto thee, then I shall bear the blame to my father for ever.

Now therefore, I pray thee, let thy servant abide instead of the lad a bondman to my lord; and let the lad go up with his brethren.

For how shall I go up to my father, and the lad be not with me? lest peradventure I see the evil that shall come on my father. (Gen. 44:18-34.)

Genesis wins us by its candor. With such moments of nobility are mingled the records of behavior contrary to the ethical standards taught elsewhere in the Law and the Prophets. It does not hide or excuse the deceit and intrigue of its heroes and heroines. Rebekah and Jacob deceive Isaac, robbing Esau of the firstborn's birthright blessing. Laban deceives Jacob by giving him Leah instead of Rachel as the reward for his seven years of labor. Jacob takes advantage of Laban by observing heredity at work in the breeding of sheep and cattle. Esau, the mistreated brother, proves to be the most magnanimous of the lot, forgiving Jacob his wrongdoing and refusing the appeasing gifts. Genesis 34 describes the deception and killing carried out by Jacob's sons to avenge the rape of their sister. Genesis 38 recounts the adultery of Judah, who was ready to burn his daughter-in-law until he found out that he was the father of her child. The daughters of Lot, driven out of Sodom and husbandless, made their father drunk and conceived by him.

Genesis is a record of human beings — violent, lustful, quarrelsome, jealous, and greedy. And yet God found these people worthy of being a covenant people. What greater encouragement could we have, in our moments of discouragement and unworthiness, than to turn to the record of Genesis and its reminder that, whatever human vagaries, the standards of God and also the steadfastness of God do not waver?

166

GENERAL INDEX

SCRIPTURE INDEX

169